The Zen Teachings of Master Lin-chi

The Zen Teachings of Master Lin-chi

A TRANSLATION OF THE LIN-CHI LU

BY BURTON WATSON

COLUMBIA UNIVERSITY PRESS
New York

Columbia University Press
Publishers Since 1893
New York   Chichester, West Sussex
Copyright 1993 Burton Watson
Preface copyright 1999 Burton Watson
All rights reserved

Library of Congress Cataloging-in-Publication Data

I-hsüan, d. 867
[Lin-chi lu.   English]
The Zen teachings of Master Lin-chi: a translation of
the Lin-chi lu/by Burton Watson.
p.   cm.
Originally published: Boston: Shambhala, 1993.
ISBN 0-231-11484-2   —   0-231-11485-0 (paper)
1. Zen Buddhism—Early works to 1800.
I. Title.
BQ9399.I554L5513   1993   98-38759
294.3'85—dc21   CIP

Casebound editions of Columbia University Press books are printed
on permanent and durable acid-free paper.
Printed in the United States of America
c 10 9 8 7 6 5 4 3 2 1
p 10 9 8 7 6 5 4

To the memory of my teacher,
Meguro Zekkai Roshi
(1908–1990)

Contents

Preface

Shout for shout, shout for shout for shout—
that instant tells if it's life or death!
Wicked devil, his ogre eyeballs
bright, bright as any sun or moon!

So goes a poem written by the Japanese Zen master Ikkyū
to inscribe on a portrait of the Chinese Zen master Lin-chi.

Who is this Lin-chi, with his devilish face and fearfully
glaring eyes, and what is he shouting about? Anyone who
takes a serious interest in Zen Buddhist teachings will probably find himself asking that question at some point, for
there is little chance of getting around Lin-chi if one hopes
to get at Zen.

His portrait, with those penetrating eyes, will confront you
everywhere in the Zen world, and when your teachers have
tired of haranguing you—"Straighten your back!" "Dig into
your koan!"—they are certain to open the book that bears
his name and harangue you further with readings from his
golden words.

Why must we listen to these pronouncements of Lin-chi?
Because his is the oldest and most authentic voice that has
come down to us from the early tradition of Chinese Ch'an
or Zen, the fullest exposition of its teachings, particularly as
they are associated with the line of transmission that honors
his name, the Lin-chi or Rinzai school of Zen. The early

figures in the Zen lineage in China who precede him are veiled in legend, their sayings fragmentary and often difficult to interpret. The later masters for the most part do little more than reiterate or embroider on Lin-chi's words and doctrines. It is the *Lin-chi lu* or *Recorded Sayings of the Ch'an Master Lin-chi*, the book made up of his sermons and descriptions of his life and his encounters with other Zen masters and students, that preserves for us the most authoritative and influential account of the basic principles and practices of Zen Buddhism in China. And this Chinese Zen in time became the parent of Korean and Japanese Zen, and of the Zen that today has spread around the world.

Lin-chi glares at us because he wants us to attend to his words, words that are of life-and-death significance. He shouts because he hopes to wake us to their meaning.

Burton Watson
April 1998

Translator's Introduction

THE SCHOOL OF Mahayana Buddhism known as Ch'an, or Zen, because it emphasizes the active expression of enlightenment over matters of doctrine, has from its early days in China assiduously compiled records of the actual words and actions of its outstanding leaders, or Ch'an masters. It is these works, known as *yü-lu,* or "recorded sayings," rather than the sutras and scholastic treatises of Mahayana Buddhism, that later followers of the school have looked to when they sought to understand and recapture the living spirit of Ch'an.

The work translated here, the *Lin-chi ch'an-shih yü-lu,* or *Recorded Sayings of Ch'an Master Lin-chi,* often referred to simply as the *Lin-chi lu,* contains extensive descriptions of the life and teachings of Lin-chi I-hsüan (d. 866), one of the greatest and most influential of the T'ang period Ch'an masters. The text, dubbed the "king" of the *yü-lu,* or "recorded sayings," genre, represents the final major formulation of Ch'an thought in China and, as Yanagida Seizan, a leading Japanese authority on Ch'an history, has noted, presents an account of Lin-chi and his teachings that is "unparalleled in Ch'an literature for its vividness and forcefulness."[1] The work is particularly significant because, though other schools or teaching lines of early Chinese Ch'an eventually died out, that founded by Lin-chi prospered and in time became the dominant school throughout China. It was one of two schools of Chinese Ch'an introduced to Japan in the thirteenth century, where it continues in existence today and from whence it has in recent years spread to many other countries of the world. For all those down through the centuries and today who adhere to the teachings of Lin-chi, or Rinzai, as he is known in Japan, the *Recorded Sayings of Ch'an Master Lin-chi* is a text of prime importance.

According to traditional accounts, the Ch'an teachings were introduced to China by a monk from India named Bodhidharma who arrived in south China late in the fifth or early in the sixth century and later made his way to the north. He is thus looked on as the First Patriarch of the school in China.

Bodhidharma was almost certainly an actual historical personage, but his life is so shrouded in legend that we can say almost nothing about him or his teachings. The same holds true for the disciples who succeeded him and carried on the teaching line in the early years of the school. It is really only with the Sixth Patriarch in the line, a monk from south China named Hui-neng (638–713), that the school began to attract wide attention and we gain a fairly clear picture of its doctrines and practices, particularly through the text known as the *Platform Sutra of the Sixth Patriarch*.[2] By this time there were already various branches of Ch'an teaching in existence, one of which, known as the Northern School, enjoyed considerable popularity among the aristocracy and officials in the T'ang capitals at Lo-yang and Ch'ang-an. But this school died out, and thereafter all branches of Ch'an teaching traced their lineage back to the Southern School represented by the Sixth Patriarch, Hui-neng.

In the early years of the T'ang dynasty, founded in 618, the

Chinese Buddhist world was dominated by schools of Buddhism such as Fa-hsiang, Hua-yen, and Chen-yen that were centered in the great temples of the capitals and enjoyed the patronage of the aristocracy, and at times that of the rulers themselves. These schools tended to be elitist in nature, their doctrines complex and difficult to master and of a kind that held little appeal for the populace as a whole.

In 755 an ambitious military leader initiated a revolt known as the An Lu-shan Rebellion that plunged the nation into armed strife and came near to overthrowing the dynasty. The capitals were seized by the rebel forces and the ruler and his court fled into exile, and though the insurgents were in time driven back, the nation continued to be racked by internal warfare until 763. The rebellion permanently weakened the power of the central government, particularly its ability to control outlying areas, and thereafter many such areas functioned as virtually independent political units. It also inflicted a severe blow on the schools of Buddhism that were centered in the capitals and had depended on the support of the ruler and the aristocracy, which included the Northern School of Ch'an mentioned earlier.

The Southern School of Ch'an, however, with its centers all located in outlying regions, escaped the worst effects of the rebellion and was able to continue the development and propagation of its teachings. Among the outstanding leaders in this period, often called the Golden Age of Chinese Ch'an, was Ma-tsu Tao-i (709–788), a disciple of a disciple of the Sixth Patriarch, who also seems to have had connections with the Northern School. When Lin-chi mentions the teaching line with which he himself is affiliated, he traces it back to Ma-tsu, and Ma-tsu thus holds a place of special importance in the Lin-chi lineage.

In the descriptions of the teaching methods of Ma-tsu and other Ch'an masters of the time, we find mention of the paradoxical verbal exchanges between student and master, the shouts and blows, and other seemingly irrational or violent actions that have become so famous a part of Ch'an, or Zen, lore. Ma-tsu was said to have been the first to shout at his students, roaring out a syllable pronounced *ho* in modern Chinese but something like *khat* in T'ang-period pronunciation. (The Japanese reading of the character, *katsu,* preserves something of the older sound.) Another master of the period, Te-shan (780–865), initiated the practice of carrying a stick with which to administer blows to his students. Both shouts and blows, as the reader will observe, are an integral part of Lin-chi's teaching technique. More will be said of their function when we come to a discussion of Lin-chi's doctrines.

As for the life of Lin-chi, or what can be known of it from the various accounts in early Ch'an works and from information contained in the *Lin-chi lu* itself, all sources agree that he was a native of Ts'ao District in the far western corner of present-day Shantung Province, the area just south of the Yellow River known in T'ang times as Ho-nan. His family name was Hsing. There is no record of just when he was born, but Yanagida, in the article cited in note 1 above, estimates that it was probably between 810 and 815.

We do not know when or under what circumstances he became a Buddhist monk, though it was presumably at a fairly early age. He himself states, in the sermon recorded in section 19 of the *Lin-chi lu,* that he first devoted himself to a study of the *vinaya,* or rules for monastic discipline, and the various sutras and treatises. He thus had a sound knowledge of the scriptures of traditional Mahayana Buddhism, as indeed is demonstrated by his frequent allusions to such writings. Later, he tells us, he grew dissatisfied with these studies and turned his attention to Ch'an.

At this time it was customary for monks who were seriously interested in Ch'an to travel about the country visiting various monasteries and listening to the preaching of different Ch'an masters until they found a teacher and locale that seemed to fit their particular needs. This is evidently what Lin-chi did, leaving his native region and journeying to the area south of the Yangtze. When we hear of him next, he is a member of the group of monks gathered about a master referred to in the *Lin-chi lu* as Huang-po.

As so often in Ch'an texts, the designation by which a master is commonly known is in fact the name of the temple or mountain where he resided. Huang-po is a mountain in the vicinity of Hung-chou in Kiangsi, a center of Ch'an activity at this time, and the master under whom Lin-chi first studied was Hsi-yün (d. ca. 850) of Mount Huang-po. Hsi-yün was a Dharma heir of Po-chang Huai-hai (720–814), who in turn was a Dharma heir of Ma-tsu Tao-i.

According to the account in section 48 of the *Lin-chi lu,* Lin-chi had been a member of Huang-po's group for three years but had never requested a private interview with the master, as he did not know what sort of question to pose if granted such an interview. At the urging of the monk in charge of the group, however, he did in time request an interview and asked Huang-po to explain to him the real meaning of Buddhism. Before he had finished speaking, the master struck him with his stick. This procedure was repeated three times, whereupon Lin-chi, concluding that bad karma from the past was hopelessly impeding his efforts at understanding, decided to withdraw from the group and go elsewhere.

Huang-po, approving this decision, urged him to go study under a master named Ta-yü.

Ta-yü, who was living in a mountain retreat in the same region, had apparently studied under Ma-tsu Tao-i and was a Dharma heir of Kuei-tsung Chih-ch'ang, a Dharma heir of Ma-tsu, but nothing more is known of him. Under Ta-yü, Lin-chi finally achieved enlightenment. The entries in the *Lin-chi lu* seem to indicate that he returned to Huang-po's temple and remained in the area for some time, though other sources suggest that he stayed with Ta-yü until the latter's death, or perhaps traveled back and forth between the two masters.

In 845 the T'ang ruler Emperor Wu-tsung, who had earlier manifested signs of anti-Buddhist sentiment, decided for various economic and ideological reasons to adopt strong measures to curtail the wealth and power of the Buddhist institutions in China. Several earlier rulers in Chinese history had taken steps to suppress the religion, charging the monastic communities with idleness, excessive wealth, and moral laxity. But the persecution initiated by Emperor Wu-tsung, though it lasted only about a year, was more severe and widespread in its effectiveness than any of those suffered by Chinese Buddhism in earlier times. Large numbers of monks and nuns were ordered to return to lay life, and thousands of temples and monasteries were destroyed. Chinese Buddhism as a whole never fully recovered from the blow, though Ch'an, because its centers were in outlying areas, seems to have been less drastically affected than were the other sects. Lin-chi was presumably in the region of Hung-chou when the persecution took place, but as there is no allusion to it among the sources dealing with his life, we may suppose that he was not directly affected, perhaps because he was at that time residing at Ta-yü's place in the mountains.

One of the distinctive features of Ch'an monastic life was the fact that the monks worked to grow at least part of their own food rather than depend entirely on alms and support from the community, as had been the custom in earlier Buddhism. In the *Lin-chi lu* we see Lin-chi working in the fields with the other monks while he was a member of Huang-po's group, or going at Huang-po's request to deliver a letter to another monastery. He also traveled around the country visiting many other Ch'an centers and meeting with the masters there.

Eventually he returned to north China, settling in Chen-chou, the city that headed the district of the same name, the present-day Cheng-ting in Hopeh Province. There he took up residence in a small temple located on the Hu-t'o River named Lin-chi-yüan, or "The Monastery Overlooking the Ford," from which he took the name Lin-chi.

By this time the ability of the T'ang to exercise effective rule was faltering badly, the nation increasingly plagued by strife and unrest, and in 907, some forty years after Lin-chi's death, the dynasty collapsed entirely, plunging China into fifty years of political disunity. The harsh and troubled nature of the period in which Lin-chi lived perhaps helps in part to account for the radical tenor of his teachings and the urgent, almost militant manner in which he proclaims them.

The episodes in the *Lin-chi lu* are not arranged in chronological order but grouped by subject, and in the very first narrative we see Lin-chi in Chen-chou, lecturing to a group of monks and lay believers at the request of a certain official named Wang—the head of the *fu,* or prefecture, in which Chen-chou was located—and the other officials in his staff.

Ch'an, because of its strong emphasis on the accessibility of enlightenment to all persons, and the simple and direct nature of its teachings, clearly had considerable popular appeal for the men and women of the time, and we frequently read of Ch'an masters being requested to expound its doctrines for the benefit of local officials and other lay believers.

Members of the Wang family, one of whom asked Lin-chi to lecture, held the post of *chieh-tu-shih,* or military governor, of the prefecture in which Chen-chou was situated for several generations and, because of the weakness of the central government, conducted themselves as virtually independent rulers of the region. Yanagida suggests that the particular Wang who requested Lin-chi to lecture on at least two occasions was Wang Shao-i, who served as military governor from 857 until his death in 866.

Another important figure in Lin-chi's life during his period of residence in Chen-chou was the Ch'an monk P'u-hua, who was apparently living in the city already when Lin-chi arrived. He was a disciple of a master who in turn had been a Dharma heir of Ma-tsu Tao-i, but little else is known of him except that he was noted for his eccentric behavior, exemplified, for example, by the bizarre account of his death recorded in section 47 of the *Lin-chi lu.*

According to the brief biography of Lin-chi in section 69 of the same text, Lin-chi, for reasons that are not stated, left Chen-chou and "went south until he reached Ho Prefecture." The ambiguous term *Ho Prefecture* has usually been taken to refer to Ho-nan, the region just south of the Yellow River where Lin-chi was born. Yanagida, however, surmises that it refers to the prefecture of Ho-chung farther to the west in the bend of the Yellow River in present-day Shansi, citing evidence to show that Lin-chi had been invited there by the military governor of the region. Wherever it was he journeyed south to, he did not stay for long but soon returned to the area north of the Yellow River and took up residence in a temple in the southern part of present-day Hopeh that belonged to Hsing-hui Ts'un-chiang (830–888), his Dharma heir and the Second Patriarch of the Lin-chi school, who carefully attended him until his death. Section 69 of the *Lin-chi lu* gives the date of Lin-chi's death as the tenth day of the first month of Hsien-t'ung 8, a date that corresponds to February 18, 867, by the Western calendar. But the earliest biography of Lin-chi, that in chapter 19 of the *Chodang chip (Tsu-t'ang chi)* gives it as the tenth day of the fourth month of Hsien-t'ung 7, which would correspond to May 27, 866. Yanagida believes that the latter date is more plausible. Lin-chi was probably in his mid-fifties when he died.

Although Ch'an often characterizes itself as a teaching that is not dependent on the written word but represents a separate transmission outside the scriptures, it is clear that the early Ch'an masters were well versed in the sutras and other texts of Mahayana Buddhism and refer to them frequently in their teachings, no doubt expecting their students to have a similar familiarity with such texts. Thus, for the benefit of readers who are not specialists in Buddhism, a few of the most important beliefs and assumptions that underlie Mahayana Buddhism are outlined here.

The doctrine of karma, which Buddhism took over from earlier Indian thought, is fundamental to its system of beliefs. According to this doctrine, all the moral acts of an individual, whether good or evil, have an inevitable effect on the individual's life and well-being, though it may require more than a single lifetime or existence for the effects to become fully apparent. Buddhism teaches that all beings are destined to undergo an endless cycle of births and deaths in six realms of existence, which are arranged in ascending order in terms of their desirability. Lowest of the six is hell, or the realm of hell-dwellers, where beings undergo painful tortures until they have expiated the guilt acquired through evil actions in the past. Above that is the realm of hungry ghosts, beings who are tormented by unending hunger and craving, and above that the realm of animals or beings of bestial nature. These three constitute the so-called three evil paths of existence.

Next is the level of the *asuras,* demons portrayed in Indian mythology as engaged in constant angry warfare, often with the god Indra. Above that is the world of human beings. Sixth and highest of all is the realm of the gods, or heavenly beings, who live longer and happier lives than beings on the other levels, but, like them, are destined in time to die and undergo transmigration. One may move up or down in these various levels, depending on the good or bad acts one performs in previous existences. But without the salvation of the Dharma, or Law—the enlightening truth of Buddhism—one can never escape from the cycle.

Above these six realms, or paths, of unenlightened beings, often referred to as the threefold world, is the region of those who have gained emancipation through the power of religious understanding. In Mahayana Buddhism this is made up of four levels, or "holy states." Lowest is that of the arhat, or saint, of Hinayana Buddhism, who has achieved a certain understanding of the Dharma but has stopped short of full enlightenment. Above the arhats are the *pratyekabuddhas,* or solitary sages, persons who have achieved a degree of understanding through their own efforts but make no attempt to teach it to others. Next are the bodhisattvas, beings who are assured of attaining full enlightenment but who, out of their great compassion, remain in the world in order to assist others. On the tenth and highest level are the buddhas, beings of perfect wisdom and enlightenment.

Lin-chi, as we will see when we come to read his sermons, often seems to be rejecting these conventional beliefs of Buddhism, or at least urging his students not to be unduly concerned with them. But one must have some knowledge of the conventional beliefs, if only to understand what is involved in their rejection. These concepts and technical terms of Buddhism will be explained further in footnotes as they occur in the translation, and the more important of them are also defined in the glossary found at the end of the book.

One more key concept of Mahayana Buddhism must be touched on here, a concept that is crucial to Lin-chi's entire doctrine. This is the concept of *shunyatā*—emptiness, or nondualism. Mahayana Buddhism in its writings manifests a profound distrust of words, insisting that the highest truth or reality can never be formulated or conveyed through verbal teachings, and Ch'an masters will be found repeatedly harping on this theme. When Mahayana texts designate the absolute, or highest truth, as emptiness, they mean that it is empty of any characteristics by which we might describe it. This is because it is a single, undifferentiated whole, and the moment we begin applying terms to it, we create dualisms that immediately do violence to that unity. Hence even the term *emptiness* itself must in the end be rejected, since it implies that there is something outside of emptiness that is not empty.

If reality is a single, all-embracing oneness, with nothing

whatsoever outside it, then the entire phenomenal world as we know and perceive it, all time and all space, must be included within that unity. In the end, then, the absolute must be synonymous with the relative or phenomenal world; or, as the *Heart Sutra* puts it, "Form is emptiness, emptiness is form." But just how are these two aspects related, how can we move or see from one aspect to the other?

Buddhism declares that the mind in a sense creates the whole phenomenal world, as a painter creates a painting with lines and colors. Without going into all the implications of this statement, it is enough here to note that the mind, in its unenlightened state, when it perceives the phenomenal world through the senses, inevitably identifies certain phenomena as desirable and others as hateful or frightening, and this gives rise to the craving and repulsion that are the source of all our sufferings. The mind thus "creates" the world in the sense that it invests the phenomenal world with value. The remedy to this situation, according to Buddhism, is to still the mind, to stop it from making discriminations and nurturing attachments toward certain phenomena and feelings of aversion toward others. When this state of calmness of mind is achieved, the darkness of ignorance and passion will be dispelled and the mind can perceive the underlying unity of the absolute. The individual will then have achieved the state of enlightenment and will be freed from the cycle of birth and death, because such a person is now totally indifferent to them both.

This is the state of understanding or awakening to which Lin-chi in his sermons is attempting to lead his listeners. He talks constantly about stilling the thoughts or of preventing thoughts from arising. He of course does not mean that one should attempt to halt the activity of the mind entirely—such a state would be attainable only in profound sleep or death. What he means is that one should try to stop the mind from making the kinds of discrimination that lead to craving or attachment.

Lin-chi's listeners, it would appear, are either monks and nuns who have already entered the Buddhist Order or lay believers with a deep interest in Buddhism. They have presumably already freed themselves from preoccupation with the commoner cravings for sensual indulgence, material gain, or worldly fame, and have entered the path of religious striving. But it is precisely this fact that Lin-chi sees as the source of their problem.

The scriptures of earlier Buddhism, the Hinayana, or Lesser Vehicle, school, as the Mahayana school derogatorily labels it, had pictured the state of Buddhahood as all but impossible for ordinary beings to attain, and taught that even to reach the arhat's level of understanding required many lifetimes of earnest endeavor. Mahayana, basing itself on its doctrine of emptiness, or nondualism, argued that, since all beings are part of a single underlying unity, they must interpenetrate one another and share each other's identity. Thus all beings must partake of the Buddha-nature and contain within themselves the "seeds" or potential for full enlightenment. But the Mahayana sutras tended to take over much of the language of earlier Buddhism and to imply that most individuals will require great effort and many lifetimes of dedication to the religious life before they can hope to reach the highest goal. A person who pursues the religious life, we are led to understand, advances by gradual stages, and though the final breakthrough to enlightenment may be sudden, it requires vast years of preparation.

The message of Lin-chi's sermons, reiterated with almost

wearisome persistence, is that his followers are allowing all this talk of goals and striving, of buddhas and patriarchs, to cloud their outlook and to block the path of understanding. All such words and concepts are external and extraneous postulations, attachment to which is just as much a delusion and impediment as attachment to any crasser objective, such as sensual gratification or material gain. Again and again he exhorts them to put aside all such external concerns and to turn their gaze within, where the Buddha-nature inherent in all beings is to be found.

In a famous passage in section 3 of the *Lin-chi lu,* Lin-chi speaks of the "True Man with no rank" who is found in all his listeners. *True Man,* or *Real Person,* is a term borrowed from the writings of the Taoist philosopher Chuang Tzu, used here presumably because Taoism was popular in the region of north China where Lin-chi was preaching at the time. It designates a person with genuine understanding of the Tao, or the Way, and here stands for the Buddha-nature inherent in all. Though Lin-chi uses the term only once, the general concept recurs over and over in the text when he urges the members of his audience to set aside outside or superficial concerns and concentrate on what he calls "this lone brightness without fixed shape or form" that is within each of them at the very moment when they stand before him listening to his sermon on the Dharma.

What he is saying, and what the Ch'an masters all say in the end, is that one should not become unduly preoccupied with the scriptures and tenets of Buddhism, nor with the rules of conduct and devotional practices that are believed to lead one step by step along the path of spiritual advancement. Nor, for that matter, is one to become preoccupied with the teachings of the Ch'an sect itself, with the words that Lin-chi himself is speaking at the moment. Indeed, we see him frequently having to admonish his hearers when they pounce with too great zeal and expectation on some novel phrase or term in his own discourse. All such "words and phrases" are to be put aside, and the student is to look within and to understand, once and for all, that there is no goal to be striven for because it has been won already, no place to be journeyed to because one is there right now.

From this it may be seen that the doctrine that Lin-chi expounds, that of the Buddha-nature inborn in the individual and the accessibility of enlightenment to all beings, is basically no different from that found in the major Mahayana sutras such as the *Lotus* and the *Vimalakirti*. What is different in the *Lin-chi lu* and the other Ch'an writings is the language in which it is expressed, and the strong emphasis on the immediacy of enlightenment and the supreme importance of the experience itself. Gone is the swooning rhetoric of the Indian sutras, the lush descriptions of jewel-adorned Buddhalands, the breathtaking expanses of time and space so vast they defy calculation. Instead we have Lin-chi's brisk, barking sentences in the colloquial language of the period, earthy, at times coarse or vulgar in expression, calling on his listeners to turn to and experience this "True Man without rank" who is within reach of them right now. Once they have done that, once they have experienced true enlightenment and broken through the barrier of ignorance into the undifferentiated realm of Emptiness, then nothing more will be required of them. They will be persons with "nothing to do," not idle, of course, since daily activities never cease, but pursuing no purposive goal, reaching out for no distant ideal, accepting all experience as it comes to them and no longer being pushed around or led astray by their surroundings.

Lin-chi seems to imply that the only thing preventing his students from attaining immediate enlightenment is their own lack of faith in their ability to do so, and their mistaken preoccupation with the externals of the religion. But of course he and the other Ch'an masters fully recognize that no amount of preaching and pronouncement can do more than lead one to the threshold of understanding; it can never ensure that one will cross over. Therefore we see them employing other methods in an effort to help their students to make the leap into enlightenment.

Sitting in meditation is of course one of the most important practices of the Ch'an school, and in the *Lin-chi lu* we catch glimpses of Lin-chi and other figures in the narrative thus engaged. Indeed, the Chinese name of the school, Ch'an, is a transcription of *dhyāna,* the Sanskrit word for meditation. It should be noted, however, that Lin-chi at one point implies that meditation as well, if too earnestly pursued with an objective in mind, can become as much an impediment as inordinate attention to any of the other external trappings of the religion.

A second teaching technique much in evidence in the *Lin-chi lu* and other early Ch'an texts is the interview between the student and the master. The protocol for such interviews was probably not at this time nearly as formalized as it became in later Ch'an practice, but consisted of a simple exchange of greetings and remarks between the two. In answer to a student's query about the nature of reality or the true meaning of Buddhism, we often find the teacher replying with a seemingly quite unrelated comment or irrational utterance. Since the ultimate nature of reality is in the end incapable of formulation in words, the teacher is attempting to convey this fact to the student, to jar the student's mind loose from its dependence on language and intellectual comprehension.

At other times, rather than resort to verbal response, the teacher may deliver a shout, a kick, or a blow with a stick. Such actions are not intended primarily as chastisements, though admittedly the Ch'an school, particularly the branch associated with Lin-chi's name, seems to delight in creating an atmosphere of tension and violence. The principal point, however, is that when one is the recipient of a blow or a shout, one experiences it immediately, inescapably, without the slightest interval during which intellection or volition might interpose themselves. It is this quality of the immediacy of the experience that the teacher is endeavoring to convey to the student, urging the student to experience the content of enlightenment in the same sudden and immediate manner.

In reading of these "Dharma battles," as they are called, these baffling exchanges of strange utterances, shouts, and blows, the reader may feel that there is some secret to it all that he is not being let in on. Such is not the case. The compilers of these Ch'an texts did not feel it necessary or advisable to append any explanation of the significance of the action. Later commentators have sometimes offered their opinion as to which participant in the exchange came out ahead or demonstrated superior understanding, but these are almost certainly no more than educated guesses, not explanations based on traditions handed down from the period when the texts were first compiled. We should probably not worry about who, if anyone, came out ahead in these exchanges, but look upon them as dynamic, perhaps even playful, manifestations of the spirit of freedom and vigor that characterizes Ch'an enlightenment.

At still other times we see Lin-chi for the moment setting aside the lofty and deliberately paradoxical language associated with the nondualistic view of reality and urging his students to search diligently for a suitable teacher and work hard to gain enlightenment, as he assures us he himself did in his youth. At such times he does not hesitate to speak in terms of goals and endeavors, the very terminology he at other times deplores. One feels it is indicative of his stature as a teacher that, rather than troubling over such petty inconsistencies, he should be willing to admit frankly to his students that enlightenment in fact *is* something to be struggled over, long and mightily in most cases, and that it looks easy only when one has broken through to the other side.

Scholarly studies on the history of Ch'an, or Zen, when describing the thought of the *Lin-chi lu,* customarily devote considerable space to various technical terms that appear in the text, such as Lin-chi's "four procedures," "three vital seals," "four shouts," and similar categories of a laconic nature. Such concepts may have been of considerable significance in Lin-chi's time and may have helped to distinguish his thought and teaching methods from those of other Ch'an masters. But from the text alone we can scarcely make out the meaning of such terms, and later commentators can offer no more than speculation to assist us. Students engaged in traditional-style Zen study must deal with them at some point, since they are used as koans, or topics for meditation, in the Rinzai school of Zen training. But readers who are interested in grasping the general significance of Lin-chi's teachings and practice will probably fare better by concentrating on the basic ideas expressed in his sermons, which are on the whole put forward in plain and forceful language, and not troubling themselves over the conundrums in the text. Taken as whole, Lin-chi's sermons represent one of the clearest and most authoritative statements that have come down to us of the tenets of the Ch'an school in its most creative period.

In section 19 of the *Lin-chi lu,* we see the master berating his students for paying inordinate attention to mere words, complaining that "in a big notebook they copy down the sayings of some worthless old fellow" like himself. He may have been only half serious in his chidings, however, since he must have known that if the students did not copy things down, no texts such as the *Lin-chi lu* would come into existence. Fortunately for us, Lin-chi's students were evidently diligent in their note taking, and not long after his death the work we know as the *Lin-chi lu* must have begun to take shape. The text as we have it now lists Lin-chi's Dharma heir Hui-jan of the San-sheng Temple as the compiler of the work, but he must surely have consulted with Lin-chi's other major disciples and associates and drawn on their notes and reminiscences of the master and his teachings.

The material in the *Lin-chi lu* is arranged by subject into four parts. The first part, entitled "Ascending the Hall," consists of short narratives in which the master is shown "ascending the hall," that is, taking the seat of honor in the lecture hall and addressing a group of monks and lay believers, or responding to questions from members of the group.

The second part, "Instructing the Group," is very similar in nature, being descriptions of sermons or addresses that Lin-chi delivered to the group of monks gathered under him for training and instruction. But the lectures are in most cases much longer than those in the first part and give full expression to all the major doctrines of Lin-chi's Dharma.

"Testing and Rating," the third part, describes encounters or interviews among Lin-chi and his students or other persons in which the participants endeavor to test one another and rate each other's level of understanding. Often they conclude with comments by other parties on the significance of the encounter.

The fourth and final part, "Record of Activities," contains narratives pertaining to Lin-chi's various activities when he was a monk in training and when he was traveling about the country. Many of these describe interviews or encounters with other Ch'an leaders that are very similar to those found in part three.

The individual narratives or sections are numbered consecutively throughout the four parts of the text, the entire work consisting of 69 sections. Though the text no doubt circulated for many years in manuscript, the earliest printed edition that we know anything about is that which came out in the second year of the Hsien-ho era of the Southern Sung, or 1120, a reprint of an earlier edition of unknown date and provenance. It bore a preface by a Sung official named Ma Fang. No copies of this 1120 edition are known to be in existence, but later editions continued to carry the Ma Fang preface, and I have included it in my translation.

In the appendix at the end of this book I have also translated two short sections pertaining to Lin-chi that are preserved in Ming editions of a Ch'an work entitled *Ku-tsun-su yü-lu* and that are sometimes included in editions of the *Lin-chi lu*. The glossary provides brief definitions of names and technical terms that occur frequently in the translation and gives full diacritical marks for Sanskrit names and terms that appear in the translation in somewhat simplified form.

My first acquaintance with the *Lin-chi lu* came in the fifties, when I was a graduate student in Chinese studies at Kyoto University and was working part-time for Mrs. Ruth Fuller Sasaki, an American student of Zen who set up in her home in Kyoto a small research center known as the First Zen Institute of America in Japan. Mrs. Sasaki's late husband, the Zen master Sasaki Sōkei-an, had some years earlier made an English translation of the *Lin-chi lu*. In order to go over the translation, improve the English style, and ready it for publication, Mrs. Sasaki organized a small study group consisting of persons who were at that time connected with the institute. The group was headed by Professor Iriya Yoshitaka, a professor of Chinese at Kyoto University and an expert in T'ang-period colloquial texts such as the *Lin-chi lu*, and Professor Yanagida Seizan of Hanazono College, a young scholar just then coming to prominence as an authority on Chinese Ch'an. The other members, in addition to Mrs. Sasaki herself, were Philip Yampolsky, the librarian of the institute and later professor of Japanese at Columbia University, the poet and Zen student Gary Snyder, and myself.

The translation, as we discovered, required a great deal of reworking, partly because of its rather awkward style, and partly because of erroneous interpretations, which Iriya and Yanagida, on the basis of their specialized knowledge, were able to correct. I left the project in 1961 and so was not involved in its later stages. Eventually several successive versions of the translation were produced, along with a vast amount of background material, but all this was as yet unpublished at the time of Mrs. Sasaki's death in 1967. In 1975 a version of the translation was finally published, though without the elaborate apparatus that Mrs. Sasaki had planned to include.[3]

The present translation was done entirely separately from that earlier version and a great many years later. I have relied mainly on the text, notes, and modern Japanese translation of Akizuki Ryūmin, *Rinzairoku,* no. 10 in the *Zen no goroku* series (Tokyo: Tsukuba shobō, 1972), and have followed the numbering of the sections in that text. Akizuki's text is based on the version originally published in China in 1120 at Mount Ku in Fu-chou. I have also consulted with great profit the text and translation by Yanagida Seizan in his *Zen goroku,* No. 18 in the *Sekai no meicho* series (Tokyo: Chūō kōronsha, 1978), pp. 181–288, and that by Iriya Yoshitaka, *Rinzairoku,* Iwanami bunko 33-310-1 (Tokyo: Iwanami shoten, 1991). I have thus been able to draw on the fine scholarship of both the experts who headed Mrs. Sasaki's project so many years ago.

Notes

1. See the English translation of an article by Yanagida, "The Life of Lin-chi I-hsüan," translated by Ruth Fuller Sasaki, *The Eastern Buddhist: New Series* 2 (1972): 70–94. The passage quoted is on page 83.

2. The text was probably compiled, at least in its original form, around 780, and was later added to. See the study and translation by Philip B. Yampolsky, *The Platform Sutra of the Sixth Patriarch* (New York: Columbia University Press, 1967).

3. Ruth Fuller Sasaki and Yoshitaka Iriya, *The Recorded Sayings of Ch'an Master Lin-chi Hui-chao of Chen Prefecture* (Kyoto: Institute for Zen Studies, Hanazono College, 1975).

The Zen Teachings of Master Lin-chi

Preface to the Recorded Sayings of Ch'an Master Lin-chi Hui-chao of Chen-chou[1]

BY MA FANG,
SCHOLAR OF THE YEN-K'ANG HALL, GOLD AND
PURPLE KUANG-LU OFFICIAL, PEACE-KEEPING ENVOY
OF CHEN-TING-FU REGION, GENERAL SUPERVISOR OF
CAVALRY AND INFANTRY FORCES, DIRECTOR OF
CH'ENG-TE MILITARY PREFECTURE[2]

At Mount Huang-po Lin-chi once met with painful blows. Then he learned how to punch Ta-yü in the ribs. That garrulous old grandmother called him "Little bed-wetting devil!" Huang-po said, "This raving idiot, coming again to pull the tiger's whiskers!" In the craggy glen he planted pines to mark the road for people who come after. With his hoe he hoed the ground, and they were all but buried alive. Huang-po approved the young man, then gave himself a slap on the mouth. On leaving, the Master wanted to burn the armrest, but later he sat on the tongues [of the men of the world].[3]

"If not to Ho-nan, then back to Ho-pei," he said. In a monastery overlooking the old ford he offered salvation to those passing back and forth. He had a firm grasp on the essentials of crossing over, a steep cliff rising ten thousand spans. He took away the person, took away the environment, molding and fashioning first-rate disciples.[4] With his three dark gates and three vital seals he pounded and shaped the monks. Constantly at home, yet never ceasing to be on the road, the True Man with no rank, going in and out the gates of the face. The heads of the two halls simultaneously shouted; guest and host were perfectly obvious. Even when illumination and action are simultaneous, fundamentally there is no former or latter,[5] like a flower-shaped mirror confronting an image, an empty valley transmitting a sound. Wonderful his responses, whatever the direction, yet he leaves not the slightest trace.

He shook out his robe and went south, halting at Ta-ming. There Ts'un-chiang of the Hsing-hua Temple carried on his teachings, greeting and attending him in the eastern hall.[6] With just a brass water bottle and an iron begging bowl, he shut his door, ceased to speak to others, a pine growing old, a cloud idling, far removed in his contentment. He had not sat long gazing at the wall when it seemed the secret transmission was about to end. "My true Dharma—who to entrust it to? This blind donkey may well destroy it!"[7]

Old Yen of Yüan-chüeh now for the sake of others passes this along.[8] The text has been carefully examined and collated so that it is free of error and discrepancy. But there's still one shout left over—that one you have to figure out for yourself. You Ch'an followers equipped with eyes, may you not interpret the text wrongly!

Preface respectfully written in the Hsüan-ho era, the year *kuei-tzu* (1120), the fifteenth day of the midmonth of autumn.

Notes

1. Chen-chou in Lin-chi's time was one of four districts making up Ch'eng-te-fu, or Ch'eng-te Prefecture, also referred to as Ho-pei Prefecture. From mid-T'ang times on the region was a virtually independent political unit under the command of the local *chieh-tu-shih,* or military governor.

2. Nothing is known about Ma Fang, the Sung dynasty official who held these various impressive titles. Almost the entire preface is written in neat four-character phrases, many of them taken directly from the text. The reader may thus do well to read the text first before tackling the preface. Though adding nothing to our knowledge of the text, the preface conveniently summarizes its main events and pronouncements.

3. Perhaps the meaning should be "and sat on Huang-po's tongue."

4. The term translated "first-rate disciples" is *hsien-t'o,* an abbreviation for *hsien-t'o-p'o,* or *saindhava,* a term from chapter 9 of the *Nirvana Sutra* that is employed as a simile for a perspicacious minister or follower.

5. The meaning of the passage is uncertain, but commentators take "illumination" to be the teacher's appraisal of the nature and level of the student's understanding, and "action" to be the action he takes on the basis of that appraisal.

6. This section is based on the Pagoda Inscription in section 69.

7. An allusion to Lin-chi's transference of his teachings to San-sheng in section 68.

8. Ch'an master Yüan-chüeh Tsung-yen of Mount Ku in Fu-chou.

The Recorded Sayings of Ch'an Master Lin-chi Hui-chao of Chen-chou

COMPILED BY THE DHARMA HEIR HUI-JAN
RESIDING IN THE SAN-SHENG TEMPLE[1]

PART ONE
Ascending the Hall

1

Constant Attendant Wang, head of the prefecture, and his various officials requested the Master to step up to the lecture seat.[2]

The Master ascended the hall and said, "Today, having found it impossible to refuse, I have complied with people's wishes and stepped up to the lecture seat. If I were to discuss the great concern[3] of Buddhism from the point of view of a follower of the sect of the Ch'an patriarchs,[4] then I could not even open my mouth, and you would have no place to plant your feet. But today I have been urged to speak by the Constant Attendant, so why should I hide the principles of our sect? Perhaps there are some valiant generals here who would like to draw up their ranks and unfurl their banners. Let them prove to the group what they can do!"

A monk asked, "What is the basic meaning of Buddhism?"

The Master gave a shout.

The monk bowed low.

The Master said, "This fine monk is the kind who's worth talking to!"

Someone asked, "Master, whose style of song do you sing? Whose school of teaching do you carry on?"

The Master said, "When I was at Huang-po's place,[5] I asked a question three times and three times I got hit."

The monk started to say something. The Master gave a shout and then struck the monk, saying, "You don't drive a nail into the empty sky!"

A study director said, "The Three Vehicles and twelve divisions of the teachings make the Buddha-nature clear enough, don't they?"[6]

The Master said, "Wild grass—it's never been cut."[7]

The study director said, "Surely the Buddha wouldn't deceive people!"

The Master said, "Buddha—where is he?"

The study director had no answer.

The Master said, "Are you trying to dupe me right in front of the Constant Attendant? Step aside! You're keeping other people from asking questions!"

The Master resumed, saying, "This religious gathering today is held for the sake of the one great concern of Buddhism. Are there any others who want to ask questions? Come forward quickly and ask them!

"But even if you open your mouths, what you say will have nothing to do with that concern. Why do I say this? Because Shakyamuni said, did he not, that 'the Dharma is separate from words and writings, and is not involved with direct or indirect causes.'[8]

"It's because you don't have enough faith that today you find yourselves tied up in knots. I'm afraid you will trouble the Constant Attendant and the other officials and keep them

10

from realizing their Buddha-nature. It's best for me to withdraw."

With that he gave a shout and then said, "People with so few roots of faith—will the day ever come when they see the end of this? Thank you for standing so long."

Notes

1. Hui-jan, as mentioned in section 68, was a Dharma heir of Lin-chi. San-sheng Temple was in Chen-chou.

2. *Constant Attendant (ch'ang-shih),* an abbreviation for *Supplementary Cavalryman and Constant Attendant,* was originally an official title, but here is purely honorary. The identity of Wang, the head of the *fu,* or prefecture, is uncertain. Yanagida tentatively identifies him with Wang Shao-i, who from 857 to 866 served as *chieh-tu-shih,* or military governor, of Ch'eng-te-fu. To "ascend the hall" and "step up to the lecture seat" means to give a religious address to a group of monks or lay believers.

3. The "point" or basic meaning of Buddhism (*ta-shih* or *i-ta-shih*)—the reason that Buddha appeared in the world—a term deriving from chapter 2 of the *Lotus Sutra.*

4. I.e., the Ch'an sect.

5. Huang-po is Hsi-yün (d. ca. 850) of Mount Huang-po, a famous Ch'an master of the time.

6. A *study director (tso-chu)* is a high-ranking monk of some sect other than Ch'an who devotes himself to the study and teaching of Buddhist scriptures. The Three Vehicles and twelve divisions represent all the teachings of Buddhism. The monk is asking why there is any need for the kind of "separate transmission outside the scriptures" such as Ch'an speaks of in order to understand the Buddha-nature.

7. The statement is very laconic, but seems to refer to a person's natural state. That is, human nature just as it is constitutes the Buddha-nature; there is no need to study the scriptures.

8. The first part of the quotation derives from the *Lankavatara Sutra,* chapter 4, the latter part from the *Vimalakirti Sutra,* chapter 3.

2

The Master one day had occasion to go to the Ho-pei prefectural office. Constant Attendant Wang, head of the prefecture, requested the Master to step up to the lecture seat.

At that time Ma-yü came forward and asked, "Of the eyes of the thousand-armed thousand-eyed bodhisattva of great compassion, which is the true eye?"[1]

The Master said, "Of the eyes of the thousand-armed thousand-eyed bodhisattva of great compassion, which is the true eye? Answer me! Answer me!"

Ma-yü dragged the Master down from the lecture seat and sat in it himself.

The Master went up close to him and said, "How are you?"

Ma-yü was about to say something when the Master dragged him down from the seat and sat in it himself.

Ma-yü thereupon walked out of the gathering, and the Master stepped down from the lecture seat.

Note

1. Mount Ma-yü in P'u-chou is the place where the monk lived; his name and identity are unknown. See section 42. Kuan-yin, or Kannon, the Bodhisattva Avalokiteshvara, is often depicted with multiple arms and eyes to symbolize the bodhisattva's abundant and all-seeing compassion.

3

The Master ascended the hall and said, "Here in this lump of red flesh there is a True Man with no rank.[1] Constantly he goes in and out the gates of your face.[2] If there are any of you who don't know this for a fact, then look! Look!"

At that time there was a monk who came forward and asked, "What is he like—the True Man with no rank?"

The Master got down from his chair, seized hold of the monk and said, "Speak! Speak!"

The monk was about to say something, whereupon the Master let go of him, shoved him away, and said, "True Man with no rank—what a shitty ass-wiper!"[3]

The Master then returned to his quarters.

Notes

1. *True Man (Chen-jen)* is a Taoist term deriving from Chuang Tzu and signifying an enlightened person; it was often used in Buddhist writings as a translation for the word *buddha*.

2. "Gates of the face" means the mouth or forehead, but here it refers to the sense organs and the six senses: sight, hearing, smell, taste, touch, and intellect.

3. Literally, a "shit-wiping stick," used in place of toilet paper, which was not in use at this time. Another interpretation would make it a "lump of dried shit." The effect is the same either way.

4

The Master ascended the hall. A monk came forward and made a deep bow. The Master gave a shout.

The monk said, "Old Reverend, it would be well if you didn't try to spy on people!"

The Master said, "Then tell me, where have you gotten to?"

The monk immediately gave a shout.

Another monk asked, "What is the basic meaning of Buddhism?"

The Master gave a shout.

The monk bowed low.

The Master said, "Do you think that was a shout of approval?"

The monk said, "The countryside thieves have been thoroughly trounced!"[1]

The Master said, "What was their fault?"

The monk said, "A second offense is not permitted!"

The Master gave a shout.

The same day the head monks of the two parts of the meditation hall[2] caught sight of each other and simultaneously gave a shout.

A monk asked the Master, "In this case, was there any guest and any host, or wasn't there?"[3]

The Master said, "Guest and host are perfectly obvious!" Then the Master said, "All of you—if you want to understand what I have just said about guest and host, go ask the two head monks of the meditation hall."

With that he stepped down from the lecture seat.

Notes

1. The monk speaks as though he were a government official reporting the defeat of a band of peasant rebels.
2. The meditation hall was divided into two parts, the front hall and the rear hall.
3. That is, can one monk be said to have come out any better than the other?

5

The Master ascended the hall. A monk asked, "What is the basic meaning of Buddhism?"

The Master held his fly whisk straight up.

The monk gave a shout.

The Master struck him.

Another monk asked, "What is the basic meaning of Buddhism?"

Again the Master held his fly whisk straight up.

The monk gave a shout.

The Master also gave a shout.

The monk was about to say something, whereupon the Master hit him.

The Master said, "All of you—if it's for the sake of the Dharma, don't hesitate to sacrifice your bodies or give up your lives! Twenty years ago, when I was at Huang-po's place, I asked three times what was clearly and obviously the real point of Buddhism, and three times he was good enough to hit me with his stick.[1] It was as though he had brushed me

15

with a sprig of mugwort. Thinking of it now, I wish I could get hit once more like that. Is there anyone who can give me such a blow?"

At that time a monk stepped forward from the group and said, "I'll give you one!"

The Master picked up his stick and handed it to the monk. The monk was about to take it, whereupon the Master struck him.

Note

1. See section 48.

6

The Master ascended the hall. A monk asked, "What is meant by this matter of the sword blade?"[1]

The Master said, "Fearful! Fearful!"

The monk was about to speak, whereupon the Master struck him.

Someone asked, "How about the lay disciple Shih-shih who worked the pestle but forgot he was moving his feet — where has he gotten to?"[2]

The Master said, "Drowned in a deep spring."

The Master then said, "Whoever comes here, I never let him slip by me, but in all cases understand where he comes from.[3] If you come in a certain way, you'll just be losing track of yourself. And if you don't come in that way, you'll be tying yourself up without using a rope. Whatever hour of the day or night, don't go around recklessly passing judgments! Whether you know what you're doing or not, you'll be wrong in every case. This much I state clearly. The world is perfectly free to criticize or condemn me all it likes! Thank you for standing so long."

Notes

1. The sword of wisdom that cuts through and annihilates all discriminative thinking.
2. Shih-shih Shan-tao, an older contemporary of Lin-chi. A monk who had been forced to return to lay life during the Buddhist persecution under Emperor Wu-tsung, he remained as a *hsing-che,* or lay disciple, and worked at the temple treading a pestle to pound grain. "Where has he gotten to?" means What mental state or degree of enlightenment has he reached?
3. That is, I will understand the person's mental state or degree of enlightenment. But this passage is very obscure, and it is unclear how, if at all, it relates to the passages preceding it.

7

The Master ascended the hall and said, "One person is sitting on top of a lonely mountain peak, yet he has not removed himself from the world. One person is in the middle of the city streets, yet he has no likes or dislikes.[1] Now which one is ahead? Which one is behind? Don't think I'm talking about Vimalakirti, and don't think I'm talking about Fu Ta-shih![2] Take care."

Notes

1. Both are in the state that transcends the dualism of absolute and relative.
2. Vimalakirti, a wealthy Indian merchant who lived at the time of Shakyamuni Buddha and had a profound understanding of the Buddha's teachings, is the subject of the *Vimalakirti Sutra*. He represents the ideal lay believer. Fu Ta-shih (497–569) was a highly revered Chinese Buddhist layman. Lin-chi is saying, "Don't think I'm talking about historical figures—I'm talking about you!"

8

The Master ascended the hall and said, "One person is eternally on the road but has never left home. One person has left home but is not on the road.[1] Which one is worthy to receive the alms of human and heavenly beings?"

With that he stepped down from the lecture seat.

Note

1. It has been suggested that "the road" represents the relative and "home" the absolute, though other interpretations are possible.

9

The Master ascended the hall. A monk asked, "What is the first phrase?"[1]

The Master said, "When the three vital seals are pressed down and lifted, the vermilion stamp appears sharp on the paper. There's no room for speculation—host and guest are clearly defined."[2]

The monk asked, "What is the second phrase?"

The Master said, "Manjushri's wonderful understanding could of course not tolerate Wu-chu's questioning. Yet why should expedient means be at variance with the wisdom that cuts off delusions?"[3]

The monk asked, "What is the third phrase?"

The Master said, "Look at the puppets performing on the stage. Their every movement is controlled by the people backstage."

The Master also said, "One phrase must be supplied with three dark gates. One dark gate must be supplied with three vital seals. There are expedients, and there are activities. All of you—how do you understand this?"

He stepped down from the seat.

Notes

1. The monk is asking about the basic meaning of Buddhism, though as it becomes clear later, there are three phrases to express it rather than only one, as we might expect. This whole passage is one of the most baffling in the whole text, and it is difficult to say what it is all about, though many attempts have been made to elucidate it.

2. Speculation is that this refers in some way to the Ch'an master's testing and ranking of his students.

3. The Bodhisattva Manjushri symbolizes perfect wisdom. Wu-chu is a Chinese monk who in 767 visited Mount Wu-t'ai, sacred to Manjushri, encountered Manjushri in human form, and held a dialogue with him. Ch'an writings frequently refer to the incident. Here Manjushri represents fundamental understanding, or the absolute, while Wu-chu represents discriminatory thinking, or the relative. In one sense, fundamental wisdom transcends the kind of questioning put to it by discriminatory thinking. But in a larger sense, the two are not at variance—that is, expedient means are not incompatible with the absolute.

PART TWO

Instructing the Group

10

The Master gave an evening lecture, instructing the group as follows: "At times one takes away the person but does not take away the environment. At times one takes away the environment but does not take away the person. At times one takes away both the person and the environment. At times one takes away neither the person nor the environment."[1]

At that time a monk asked, "What does it mean to take away the person but not take away the environment?"

The Master said, "Warm sun shines forth, spreading the earth with brocade. The little child's hair hangs down, white as silk thread."[2]

The monk asked, "What does it mean to take away the environment but not take away the person?"

The Master said, "The king's commands have spread throughout the realm. Generals beyond the border no longer taste the smoke and dust of battle."[3]

The monk asked, "What does it mean to take away both the person and the environment?"

The Master said, "All word cut off from Ping and Fen — they stand alone, a region apart."[4]

The monk said, "What does it mean to take away neither the person nor the environment?"

The Master said, "The king ascends his jeweled hall; country oldsters sing their songs."[5]

Notes

1. This passage has come to be known as "Lin-chi's Four Procedures." The procedures appear to represent a series of steps in the process of Ch'an training or enlightenment: one learns to transcend distinctions of subject (person) and object (environment) until one reaches a plane where neither exists; as a final step one then returns to the level of the ordinary world. *Ching,* the world translated here as "environment," could perhaps better be rendered as "circumstances" or "surroundings" in many contexts, but I have tried to translate it as "environment" throughout because it is such a key concept in Buddhist thought.

2. A nonhuman realm of fantasy.

3. A realm in which human beings are in complete control.

4. Ping and Fen are outlying regions in northern China. In Lin-chi's time, local military governors often defied the central government and established their areas as virtually independent states. Here Ping and Fen (environment) and the central government (person) cut each other off or negate each other.

5. An ordinary, everyday, peaceful realm.

11

The Master instructed the group, saying: "Those who study the Dharma of the buddhas these days should approach it with a true and proper understanding. If you approach it with a true and proper understanding, you won't be affected by considerations of birth or death, you'll be free to go or stay as you please. You don't have to strive for benefits, benefits will come of themselves.

"Followers of the Way, the outstanding teachers from times past have all had ways of drawing people out. What I myself want to impress on you is that you mustn't be led astray by others. If you want to use this thing, then use it and have no doubts or hesitations![1]

"When students today fail to make progress, where's the fault? The fault lies in the fact that they don't have faith in themselves! If you don't have faith in yourself, then you'll be forever in a hurry trying to keep up with everything around you, you'll be twisted and turned by whatever environment you're in and you can never move freely. But if you can just stop this mind that goes rushing around moment by moment looking for something, then you'll be no different from the patriarchs and buddhas. Do you want to get to know the patriarchs and buddhas? They're none other than you, the people standing in front of me listening to this lecture on the Dharma!

"Students don't have enough faith in themselves, and so they rush around looking for something outside themselves. But even if they get something, all it will be is words and phrases, pretty appearances. They'll never get at the living thought of the patriarchs!

"Make no mistake, you followers of Ch'an. If you don't

find it in this life, then for a thousand lifetimes and ten thousand *kalpas* you'll be reborn again and again in the threefold world,[2] you'll be lured off by what you think are favorable environments and be born in the belly of a donkey or a cow!

"Followers of the Way, as I look at it, we're no different from Shakyamuni. In all our various activities each day, is there anything we lack? The wonderful light of the six faculties[3] has never for a moment ceased to shine. If you could just look at it this way, then you'd be the kind of person who has nothing to do for the rest of his life.[4]

"Fellow believers, 'There is no safety in the threefold world; it is like a burning house.'[5] This is no place for you to linger for long! The deadly demon of impermanence will be on you in an instant, regardless of whether you're rich or poor, old or young.

"If you want to be no different from the patriarchs and buddhas, then never look for something outside yourselves. The clean pure light in a moment of your mind—that is the Essence-body of the Buddha lodged in you. The undifferentiated light in a moment of your mind—that is the Bliss-body of the Buddha lodged in you. The undiscriminating light in a moment of your mind—that is the Transformation-body of the Buddha lodged in you.[6] These three types of bodies are you, the person who stands before me now listening to this lecture on the Dharma! And simply because you do not rush around seeking anything outside yourselves, you can command these fine faculties.

"According to the expounders of the sutras and treatises, the threefold body is to be taken as some kind of ultimate goal. But as I see it, that's not so. This threefold body is nothing but mere names. Or they're three types of dependencies.[7] One man of early times said, 'The body depends on doctrine for its definition, and the land is discussed in terms of the reality.'⁸ This 'body' of the Dharma-realm, or reality, and this 'land' of the Dharma-realm we can see clearly are no more than flickering lights.

"Followers of the Way, you should realize that the person who manipulates these flickering lights is the source of the buddhas, the home that all followers of the Way should return to. Your physical body made up of the four great elements⁹ doesn't know how to preach the Dharma or listen to the Dharma. Your spleen and stomach, your liver and gall don't know how to preach the Dharma or listen to the Dharma. The empty spaces don't know how to preach the Dharma or listen to the Dharma. What is it, then, that knows how to preach the Dharma or listen to the Dharma? It is you who are right here before my eyes, this lone brightness without fixed shape or form—this is what knows how to preach the Dharma and listen to the Dharma. If you can see it this way, then you'll be no different from the patriarchs and buddhas.

"But never at any time let go of this even for a moment. Everything that meets your eyes is this. But 'when feelings arise, wisdom is blocked; when thoughts waver, reality departs,'¹⁰ therefore you keep being reborn again and again in the threefold world and undergoing all kinds of misery. But as I see it, there are none of you incapable of profound understanding, none of you incapable of emancipation.

"Followers of the Way, this thing called mind has no fixed form; it penetrates all the ten directions. In the eye we call it sight, in the ear we call it hearing; in the nose it detects odors, in the mouth it speaks discourse; in the hand it grasps, in the feet it runs along. Basically it is a single bright essence, but it divides itself into these six functions. And because this single mind has no fixed form, it is everywhere in a state of emancipation. Why do I tell you this? Because you followers of the Way seem to be incapable of stopping this mind that goes rushing around everywhere looking for something. So you get caught up in those idle devices of the men of old.

"The way I see it, we should cut off the heads of the Bliss-body and Transformation-body buddhas. Those who have fulfilled the ten stages of bodhisattva practice are no better than hired field hands; those who have attained the enlightenment of the fifty-first and fifty-second stages are prisoners shackled and bound; arhats and *pratyekabuddhas* are so much filth in the latrine, *bodhi*[11] and nirvana are hitching posts for donkeys. Why do I speak of them like this? Because you followers of the Way fail to realize that this journey to enlightenment that takes three *asamkhya kalpas* to accomplish is meaningless.[12] So these things become obstacles in your way. If you were truly proper men of the Way, you would never let that happen.

"Just get so you can follow along with circumstances and use up your old karma. When the time comes to do so, put on your clothes. If you want to walk, walk. If you want to sit, sit. But never for a moment set your mind on seeking Buddhahood. Why do this way? A man of old said, 'If you try to create good karma and seek to be a buddha, then Buddha will become a sure sign you will remain in the realm of birth and death.'[13]

"Fellow believers, time is precious! You rush off frantically on side roads, studying Ch'an, studying the Way, clinging to words, clinging to phrases, seeking Buddha, seeking the patriarchs, seeking a good friend, scheming, planning. But make no mistake. Followers of the Way, you have one set of parents—what more are you looking for?[14] You should stop and take a good look at yourselves. A man of old tells us that Yajnadatta thought he had lost his head and went looking for it, but once he had put a stop to his seeking mind, he found he was perfectly all right.[15]

"Fellow believers, just act ordinary, don't affect some special manner. There's a bunch of old bald-headed fellows who can't tell good from bad but who spy gods here, spy devils there, point to the east, gesture to the west, declare they 'love' clear weather or they 'love' it when it rains. They'll have a lot to answer for one day when they stand before old Yama and have to swallow a ball of red-hot iron![16] Men and women of good family let themselves be taken in by this bunch of wild fox spirits and end up completely bewitched. Blind men, idiots! One day they'll have to pay for all the food wasted on them!"

Notes

1. I.e., if you want to put into action the power of enlightenment.
2. The realm of unenlightened beings: the worlds of desire, form, and formlessness.
3. The six senses: sight, hearing, smell, taste, touch, and intellect.
4. That is, a person who realizes he need seek nothing outside himself.
5. A quotation from chapter 3 of the *Lotus Sutra*.
6. The concept of the threefold body or three aspects of the Buddha is a fundamental doctrine in Mahayana Buddhism. The *Dharmakaya*, or Essence-body, is the Buddha as pure Dharma or suchness, transcending personality. The *Sambhogakaya*, or Bliss-body, is the Buddha endowed with infinite attributes of bliss or reward gained through his practices as a bodhisattva. The *Nirmanakaya*, or Transformation-body, is the Buddha as he appears to ordinary believers. Lin-chi is saying that all these

difficult and abstruse philosophical distinctions in the end refer to no one but yourself.

7. Versions of this passage in the *Kuang-teng lu* and *Lien-teng hui-yao* read, "Or they're three types of robes." The characters for "dependence" and for "robe" are pronounced the same and written almost alike, so there may be a deliberate play on words here. In either case, Lin-chi is saying that the distinctions of the three bodies are something superficial and imposed from the outside.

8. Lin-chi is apparently referring to a saying attributed to Tz'u-en K'uei-chi (632–682) recorded in *Fa-yüan i-lin chang* 7.

9. The four elements that in Indian thought make up the body, namely, earth, water, fire, and air. Sometimes a fifth, space, is added, representing the cavities in the body.

10. A quotation from the *Hsin Hua-yen-ching lu,* chapter 1, by Li T'ung-hsüan (639–734).

11. *Bodhi* is perfect enlightenment. In this passage, of course, Lin-chi is simply holding up to ridicule the whole elaborate technical vocabulary of traditional Buddhist thought, which he looks on as an impediment to understanding.

12. The path of the bodhisattva, with its many stages of progress toward enlightenment, which is said to require countless *kalpas* to accomplish. An *asamkhya kalpa* is an immeasurably long period of time.

13. A quotation from the "Hymns of the Mahayana" by Pao-chih (425–514), recorded in chapter 29 of the *Ching-te ch'uan-teng lu,* a work compiled in 1004 that contains biographies of Indian and Chinese Ch'an masters.

14. I.e., you have the Buddha-nature inborn in you.

15. The story is found in chapter 4 of the *Shuramgama Sutra.*

16. This passage, in very colloquial language, is an illustration of monks who "affect a special manner," commenting officiously on the weather and behaving in other eccentric ways. Yama is

the king of hell before whom the dead come to be judged and punished for their offenses.

12

The Master instructed the group, saying: "Followers of the Way, what is important is to approach things with a true and proper understanding. Walk wherever you please in the world but don't let yourselves be muddled or misled by that bunch of goblin spirits. The man of value is the one who has nothing to do.[1] Don't try to do something special, just act ordinary. You look outside yourselves, going off on side roads hunting for something, trying to get your hands on something. That's a mistake. You keep trying to look for the Buddha, but *Buddha* is just a name, a word.

"Do you know what it is that everyone is rushing around looking for? All the buddhas and patriarchs of the three existences of past, present, and future and in all the ten directions make their appearance in this world just so they can seek the Dharma. And you followers of the Way who have come to study, you are here now just so you can seek the Dharma. Once you get the Dharma, that will settle things, but until you do, you will go on as before being reborn again and again in the five paths.[2]

"What is this thing called Dharma? Dharma is the Dharma, or Truth, of the mind. The Dharma of the mind has no fixed form; it penetrates all the ten directions. It is in operation right before our eyes. But because people don't have enough faith, they cling to words, cling to phrases. They try to find the Dharma of the buddhas by looking in written words, but they're as far away from it as heaven is from earth.

"Followers of the Way, when I preach the Dharma, what Dharma do I preach? I preach the Dharma of the mind. So it can enter into the common mortal or the sage, the pure or the filthy, the sacred or the secular. But you who are sacred or secular, common mortals or sages, can't start fixing names or labels to all the others who are sacred or secular, common mortals or sages. And those sacred or secular, common mortals or sages can't fix a name or label to a person like this. Followers of the Way, get hold of this thing and use it, but don't fix a label to it. This is what I call the Dark Meaning.

"My preaching of the Dharma is different from that of other people in the world. Even if Manjushri and Samantabhadra[3] were to appear here before my eyes, each manifesting his bodily form and asking about the Dharma, they would no sooner have said, 'We wish to question the Master,' than I'd have seen right through them.

"I sit calmly in my seat, and when followers of the Way come for an interview, I see through them all. How do I do this? Because my way of looking at them is different. I don't worry whether on the outside they are common mortals or sages, or get bogged down in the kind of basic nature they have inside. I just see all the way through them and never make an error."

Notes

1. The *Pao-tsung lun,* attributed to Seng-chao (384–414) but probably of later date, states, "With regard to the Way, what is valued in every age is to have nothing to do. With regard to the Way, when one is mindless, then all things will proceed smoothly."

2. The realms of hell, hungry ghosts, animals, humans, and heavenly beings.

3. Manjushri has been described in note 3, section 9 above. Samantabhadra is another important bodhisattva of Mahayana Buddhism, the symbol of religious practice. His cult in China was especially associated with Mount Omei in Szechwan.

13

The Master instructed the group, saying: "Followers of the Way, the Dharma of the buddhas calls for no special undertakings. Just act ordinary, without trying to do anything particular. Move your bowels, piss, get dressed, eat your rice, and if you get tired, then lie down. Fools may laugh at me, but wise men will know what I mean.

"A man of old said, 'People who try to do something about what is outside themselves are nothing but blockheads.'[1] If, wherever you are, you take the role of host, then whatever spot you stand in will be a true one. Then whatever circumstances surround you, they can never pull you awry. Even if you're faced with bad karma left over from the past, or the five crimes that bring on the hell of incessant suffering, these will of themselves become the great sea of emancipation.[2]

"Students these days haven't the slightest comprehension of the Dharma. They're like sheep poking with their noses— whatever they happen on they immediately put in their mouths. They can't tell a gentleman from a lackey, can't tell a host from a guest. People like that come to the Way with twisted minds, rushing in wherever they see a crowd. They don't deserve to be called true men who have left the household.³ All they are in fact is true householders, men of secular life.

"Someone who has left household life must know how to act ordinary and have a true and proper understanding, must know how to tell buddhas from devils, to tell true from sham, to tell common mortals from sages. If they can tell these apart, you can call them true men who have left the household. But if they can't tell a buddha from a devil, then all they've done is leave one household to enter another. You might describe them as living beings who are creating karma. But you could never call them true men who have left the household.

"Suppose there were a substance made of buddhas and devils blended without distinction into a single body, like water and milk mixed together. The *hamsa* goose could drink out just the milk.⁴ But followers of the Way, if they have really keen eyes, will thrust aside buddhas and devils alike. While you love sages and loath common mortals, you're still bobbing up and down in the sea of birth and death."⁵

Notes

1. From a poem attributed to the eighth-century Ch'an master Ming-tsan, or Lan-tsan, of Mount Nan-yüeh.
2. The five crimes are usually given as (1) killing one's father, (2) killing one's mother, (3) killing an arhat, (4) doing injury to a buddha, and (5) causing dissension in the Monastic Order. Any one of these condemns the doer to suffer in the *Avichi* hell, the hell of incessant suffering.
3. *Ch'u-chia*, to leave the family or the household life, is the common term in Chinese for becoming a monk or nun.
4. According to Indian lore, the bird known as a *hamsa* is capable

of extracting milk from a mixture of milk and water and leaving the water undrunk.

5. This last sentence is quoted from the "Hymns of the Mahayana" by Pao-chih.

14

Someone asked, "What is the Buddha devil?"

The Master said, "If you have doubts in your mind for an instant, that's the Buddha devil. But if you can understand that the ten thousand phenomena were never born, that the mind is like a conjurer's trick, then not one speck of dust, not one phenomenon will exist. Everywhere will be clean and pure, and this will be Buddha. Buddha and devil just refer to two states, one stained, one pure.

"As I see it, there's no Buddha, no living beings, no long ago, no now. If you want to get it, you've already got it—it's not something that requires time. There's no religious practice, no enlightenment, no getting anything, no missing out on anything. At no time is there any other Dharma than this. If anyone claims there is a Dharma superior to this, I say it must be a dream, a phantom. All I have to say to you is simply this.

"Followers of the Way, this lone brightness before my eyes now, this person plainly listening to me[1]—this person is unimpeded at any point but penetrates the ten directions, free to do as he pleases in the threefold world. No matter what environment he may encounter, with its peculiarities and differences, he cannot be swayed or pulled awry. In the space of an instant he makes his way into the Dharma-realm. If he meets a buddha he preaches to the buddha, if he meets a patriarch he preaches to the patriarch, if he meets an arhat he preaches to the arhat, if he meets a hungry ghost he preaches to the hungry ghost. He goes everywhere, wandering through many lands, teaching and converting living beings, yet never becomes separated from his single thought. Every place for him is clean and pure, his light pierces the ten directions, the ten thousand phenomena are a single thusness.

"Followers of the Way, the really first-rate fellow knows right now that from the first there's never been anything that needed doing. It's because you don't have enough faith that you rush around moment by moment looking for something. You throw away your head and then hunt for a head, and you can't seem to stop yourselves. You're like the bodhisattva of perfect and immediate enlightenment[2] who manifests his body in the Dharma-realm but who, in the midst of the Pure Land, still hates the state of common mortal and prays to become a sage. People like that have yet to forget about making choices. Their minds are still occupied with thoughts of purity or impurity.

"But the Ch'an school doesn't see things that way. What counts is this present moment—there's nothing that requires a lot of time. Everything I am saying to you is for the moment only, medicine to cure the disease. Ultimately it has no true reality. If you can see things in this way, you will be true men who have left the household, free to spend ten thousand in gold each day.[3]

"Followers of the Way, don't let just any old teacher put his stamp of approval on your face, don't say 'I understand Ch'an! I understand the Way!' spouting off like a waterfall. All that sort of thing is karma leading to hell. If you're a person who honestly wants to learn the Way, don't go looking for the world's mistakes, but set about as fast as you can looking for a true and proper understanding. If you can acquire a true and proper understanding, one that's clear and complete, then you can start thinking of calling it quits."

Notes

1. The individual listeners in the assembly.
2. One who has reached the highest stage of bodhisattva practice.
3. That is, you will be worthy of the alms you receive.

15

Someone asked, "What do you mean by a true and proper understanding?"

The Master said, "You enter all sorts of states of the common mortal or the sage, of the stained or the pure. You enter the lands of the various buddhas, you enter the halls of Maitreya, you enter the Dharma-realm of Vairochana,[1] and everywhere all these lands are manifest, coming into being, continuing, declining, and passing into emptiness. The Buddha appears in the world, turns the wheel of the great Law, and then enters nirvana, but you cannot see any semblance of his coming and going. If you look for his birth and death, in the end you can never find it. You enter the Dharma-realm of no-birth,[2] wandering everywhere through various lands, you enter the world of the Lotus Treasury[3] and you see fully that all phenomena are empty of characteristics, that none have any true reality.

"You listening to the Dharma, if you are men of the Way who depend on nothing,[4] then you are the mother of the buddhas. Therefore the buddhas are born from the realm that leans on nothing. If you can waken to this leaning on nothing, then there will be no Buddha to get hold of. If you can see things in this way, this is a true and proper understanding.

"But students don't push through to the end. Because they seize on words and phrases and let words like *common mortal* or *sage* obstruct them, this blinds their eyes to the Way and they cannot perceive it clearly. Things like the twelve divisions of the scriptures[5] all speak of surface or external matters. But students don't realize this and immediately form their understanding on the basis of such surface and external words and phrases. All this is just depending on something, and whoever does that falls into the realm of cause and effect and hasn't yet escaped the threefold world of birth and death.

"If you want to be free to be born or die, to go or stay as one would put on or take off a garment, then you must understand right now that the person here listening to the Dharma has no form, no characteristics, no root, no beginning, no place he abides, yet he is vibrantly alive. All the ten thousand kinds of contrived happenings operate in a place that is in fact no place. Therefore the more you search the farther away you get, the harder you hunt the wider astray you go. This is what I call the secret of the matter.

"Followers of the Way, don't take up with some dream or phantom for a companion. Sooner or later you're headed for the impermanence that awaits us all. While you are in this world, what sort of thing do you look to for emancipation? Instead of just looking for a mouthful of food and spending time patching up your robe, you should go around hunting for a teacher. Don't just drift along, always trying to take the easy way. Time is precious, moment by moment impermanence draws nearer! The elements of earth, water, fire, and air are waiting to get the coarser part of you; the four phases of birth, continuation, change, and extinction press on your subtler side. Followers of the Way, now is the time to understand the four types of environment that are without characteristics.[6] Don't just let the environment batter you around."

Notes

1. Maitreya is a bodhisattva who at some far distant time in the future is destined to appear on earth as the next buddha. Vairochana is a buddha described in the *Avatamsaka,* or *Hua-yen, Sutra,* a central figure in esoteric Buddhism.

2. The realm of emptiness or nondualism where all distinctions such as birth and death are transcended.

3. The world created through the vows and practices of Vairochana Buddha, where cause and effect exist simultaneously, like the flower and seed of the lotus.

4. I.e., who have transcended all distinctions and entered the realm of nondualism.

5. The twelve sections into which the Buddhist scriptures are divided, depending on the style of exposition.

6. The characteristics of the four elements are described in chapter 18 of the *Ta-chih-tu lun* as hard and weighty for earth, cold and wet for water, hot and bright for fire, light and in motion for air. But the nondiscriminative understanding of the enlightened person renders the elements void of characteristics, hence the "four types of environment without characteristics."

16

Someone asked, "What do you mean by four types of environment without characteristics?"

The Master said, "If your mind entertains a moment of doubt, it becomes obstructed by the element earth. If your mind entertains a moment of craving, it becomes drowned in the element water. If your mind entertains a moment of anger, it is seared by the element fire. If your mind entertains a moment of delight, it is tossed about by the element air. If you can understand that this is so, however, you will not be swayed by the environment but can utilize the elements wherever you may be. You can pop up in the east and vanish in the west, pop up in the south and vanish in the north, pop up in the middle and vanish in the borderland, pop up in the borderland and vanish in the middle. You can walk on water as though it were earth, walk on earth as though it were water.[1] How can you do this? Because you understand that the four great elements are mere dreams or phantoms.

"Followers of the Way, you who are here now listening to the Dharma are not the four great elements in you, but something that can make use of the four great elements in you. If you can just see it in this way, then you will be free to go or stay.

"The way I see it, one shouldn't be averse to anything. Suppose you yearn to be a sage. Sage is just a word, *sage*. There are some types of students who go off to Mount Wu-t'ai looking for Manjushri. They're wrong from the very start! Manjushri isn't on Mount Wu-t'ai. Would you like to get to know Manjushri? You here in front of my eyes, carrying out your activities, from first to last never changing, wherever you go never doubting—this is the living Manjushri!

"Your mind that each moment shines with the light of nondiscrimination—wherever it may be, this is the true Samantabhadra. Your mind that each moment is capable of freeing itself from its shackles, everywhere emancipated— this is the method of meditating on Kuan-yin.[2] These three act as host and companion to one another, all three appearing at the same time when they appear, one in three, three in one.[3] Only when you have understood all this will you be ready to read the scriptural teachings."

Notes

1. The scriptures describe persons possessed of supernatural powers who can perform such feats as Lin-chi mentions here. His words are meant simply to symbolize the freedom enjoyed by the person of correct understanding.
2. The method of calling on the saving power of the Bodhisattva Avalokiteshvara, or Kuan-yin, described in chapter 25 of the *Lotus Sutra*.
3. The three bodhisattvas represent wisdom (Manjushri), religious practice (Samantabhadra), and compassion (Kuan-yin). At different times one or the other takes the leading role, with the other two acting as attendants.

17

The Master instructed the group, saying: "Those who study the Way these days need to have faith in themselves and not go looking for something outside. Otherwise they get caught up in foolish and trifling environments and can't even tell crooked from straight. There are patriarchs and there are buddhas, but those are all just things found in the scriptural teachings. Someone comes along with a phrase he has picked up, brings it out in a manner that's half clear, half murky, and at once you start having doubts, looking at the sky, looking at the ground, running off to ask somebody else, getting into a great flurry. If you want to be first-rate fellows, don't go around talking about the ruler or the rebels, talking about right and wrong, talking about sex and money matters, spending all your days talking idle chatter!

"Here at my place we don't talk about who is a monk and who is a lay believer. When someone comes to me, I can tell exactly what he is like. Whatever circumstances he may have come from, I take all his words and utterances to be so many dreams and phantoms. But when I see a man who has learned to master the environment, I know that here is the secret meaning of the buddhas.

"A man in a Buddha environment, or state of enlightenment, can't announce himself, saying, 'I'm in a Buddha environment.' But a man of the Way who has learned to lean on nothing is master of the environment when he appears. If this kind of man appears and says to me, 'I'm looking for the Buddha,' I respond at once by meeting him with a clean and pure environment. If a man asks me about bodhisattvas, I respond at once by meeting him with an environment of pity and compassion. If a man asks me about *bodhi,* I respond at once by meeting him with an environment of wonderful purity. If a man asks me about nirvana, I respond at once by meeting him with an environment of stillness and tranquillity. The environment takes ten thousand different shapes, but the person never varies. Therefore in response to the object he manifests different forms, like the moon in the water.[1]

"Followers of the Way, if you want to be constantly in accord with the Dharma, you'll have to begin by learning to be first-rate fellows. Be weak-kneed and wishy-washy and you'll never get there. No vessel with cracks in it is fit to hold ghee.[2] If you want to be a truly great vessel, you must never be led astray by others. Wherever you are, play the host and then any place you stand will be a true one.

"Whatever confronts you, don't let yourself be imposed on. If you entertain even a moment of doubt, the devil will enter your mind. Even a bodhisattva, when he starts doubting, is prey to the devil of birth and death. Learn to put a stop to thoughts and never look for something outside yourselves. When an object appears, shine your light on it. Just have faith in this thing that is operating in you right now. Outside of it, nothing else exists.

"Your mind in one moment of thought creates the threefold world. Depending on conditions, you experience its various environments, and it divides itself to become the six dusts.[3] In the way you now respond and utilize it, what do you lack? In the space of an instant you enter purity or enter defilement, enter the halls of Maitreya or enter the lands of the three eyes.[4] You wander at ease everywhere, for you see that these are all empty names."

Notes

1. Probably an allusion to the passage in "Verses of the Four Heavenly Kings" in chapter 2 of the *Chin-kuang-ming Sutra:*

"The true Essence-body of the Buddha is like empty space. In response to the object it manifests different forms, like the moon in the water."

2. Ghee, the finest clarified butter, is used in Buddhist literature to symbolize the highest level of the teachings.

3. The six senses.

4. The "lands of the three eyes" is explained in the section that follows.

18

Someone asked, "What do you mean by the lands of the three eyes?"[1]

The Master said, "You and I together enter the land of wonderful purity, put on clean pure robes, and preach the Buddha of the Essence-body. Again we enter the land of non-discrimination, put on the robes of nondiscrimination, and preach the Buddha of the Bliss-body. Or again we enter the land of emancipation, put on the robes of shining brightness, and preach the Buddha of the Transformation-body. But these lands of the three eyes are all just a change in the dependent condition, a change of robe.[2]

"According to the expounders of the sutras and treatises, we should regard the Essence-body as the root of reality and the Bliss-body and Transformation-body as its functions. But as I see it, the Essence-body, or Dharma-body, is incapable of preaching the Dharma.[3] Therefore a man of old said, 'The body depends on the doctrine for its definition, and the land is discussed in terms of its reality.' The Dharma-realm body, the Dharma-realm land—we can see clearly that these are mere concocted things, trumped-up lands, an empty fist, a yellow leaf one uses to divert a little child. What juice can you expect to get from the spines of brambles or caltrops or from old dried bones? Outside the mind there is no Dharma, and even inside the mind it can't be grasped. So what is there to seek for?

"You go all over the place, saying, 'There's religious practice, there's enlightenment.' Make no mistake! If there were such a thing as religious practice, it would all be just karma keeping you in the realm of birth and death. You say, 'I observe all the six rules[4] and the ten thousand practices.' In my view all that sort of thing is just creating karma. Seeking Buddha, seeking the Dharma—that's just creating karma that leads to hell. Seeking the bodhisattvas—that too is creating karma. Studying sutras, studying doctrine—that too is creating karma. The buddhas and patriarchs are people who don't have anything to do. Hence, whether they have defilements and doings or are without defilements and doings, their karma is clean and pure.

"There are a bunch of blind baldheads who, having stuffed themselves with rice, sit doing Ch'an-style meditation practice, trying to arrest the flow of thoughts and stop them from arising, hating clamor, demanding silence—but these aren't Buddhist ways! The Patriarch Shen-hui said: 'If you try to arrest the mind and stare at silence, summon the mind and focus it on externals, control the mind and make it clear within, concentrate the mind and enter into meditation, all practices of this sort create karma.'[5] You, this person who is right now listening to the Dharma here—how would you have him practice, how enlighten him, how adorn him? He's not the sort of fellow who can be expected to carry out practices, not the sort who can be adorned. If you wanted to adorn him, you'd have to adorn him with everything that exists. Make no mistake about this!

"Followers of the Way, you take the words that come out of the mouths of a bunch of old teachers to be a description of the true Way. You think, 'This is a most wonderful teacher and friend. I have only the mind of a common mortal, I would never dare try to fathom such venerableness.' Blind idiots! You go through life with this kind of understanding, betraying your own two eyes, cringing and faltering like a donkey on an icy road, saying, 'I would never dare speak ill of such a good friend, I'd be afraid of making mouth karma!'

"Followers of the Way, the really good friend is someone who dares to speak ill of the Buddha, speak ill of the patriarchs, pass judgment on anyone in the world, throw away the *Tripitaka*,⁶ revile those little children, and in the midst of opposition and assent search out the real person. So for the past twelve years, though I've looked for this thing called karma, I've never found so much as a particle of it the size of a mustard seed.⁷

"Those Ch'an masters who are as timid as a new bride are afraid they might be expelled from the monastery or deprived of their meal of rice, worrying and fretting. But from times past the real teachers, wherever they went, were never listened to and were always driven out—that's how you know they were men of worth. If everybody approves of you wherever you go, what use can you be? Hence the saying, Let the lion give one roar and the brains of the little foxes will split open.

"Followers of the Way, here and there you hear it said that there is a Way to be practiced, a Dharma to become enlightened to. Will you tell me then just what Dharma there is to become enlightened to, what Way there is to practice? In your present activities, what is it you lack, what is it that practice must mend? But those little greenhorn monks don't understand this and immediately put faith in that bunch of wild fox spirits, letting them spout their ideas and tie people in knots, saying, 'When principle and practice match one another and proper precaution is taken with regard to the three types of karma of body, mouth, and mind, only then can one attain Buddhahood.' People who go on like that are as plentiful as springtime showers.

"A man of old said, 'If along the road you meet a man who is master of the Way, whatever you do, don't talk to him about the Way.'[8] Therefore it is said, 'If a person practices the Way, the Way will never proceed. Instead, ten thousand kinds of mistaken environments will vie in poking up their heads. But if the sword of wisdom comes to cut them all down, then even before the bright signs manifest themselves, the dark signs will have become bright.'[9] Therefore a man of old said, 'The everyday mind—that is the Way.'[10]

"Fellow believers, what are you looking for? This man of the Way who depends on nothing, here before my eyes now listening to the Dharma—his brightness shines clearly, he has never lacked anything. If you want to be no different from the patriarchs and buddhas, learn to see it this way and never give in to doubt or questioning. While your mind moment by moment never differentiates, it may be called the living patriarch. If the mind differentiates, its nature and manifestations become separated from one another. But so long as it does not differentiate, its nature and manifestations do not become separated."

Notes

1. The term *three eyes* usually refers to the land of the three types of eye, the Dharma eye, the eye of knowledge, and the eye of

wisdom, described in the last chapter of the *Avatamsaka Sutra,*
called "Entering the Dharma-realm." But Lin-chi relates the
term to the threefold body of the Buddha, which was described in note 6, section 11.

2. See note 7, section 11 for the relationship between robes and
   dependent conditions.

3. Because the essence, or highest truth, as represented by the
   Essence-body cannot be expressed in words.

4. The six *paramitas* that bodhisattvas must observe in order to
   attain Buddhahood: almsgiving, keeping of the precepts, forbearance, assiduousness, meditation, and wisdom.

5. Quoted from the famous attack on the practices of the Northern School of Ch'an by Ho-tse Shen-hui (670–762), the *P'u-
   t'i-ta-mo Nan-tsung ting shih-fei lun.*

6. The collected scriptures of Buddhism; but here perhaps Lin-
   chi means the teachings of Hinayana Buddhism.

7. Just why Lin-chi speaks of "twelve years" is not certain; perhaps the passage is a quotation from some unknown work.
   Iriya takes "twelve years" to mean a long time.

8. The words of Pen-ching (667–761), a disciple of the Sixth Patriarch, recorded in *Tsu-t'ang chi 3.*

9. The source of the quotation is unknown. According to Yanagida, the bright signs represent expedient or adapted wisdom,
   the dark signs, basic wisdom.

10. The words of Ma-tsu Tao-i (709–788) recorded in *Ching-te
    ch'uan-teng lu 28,* biography of Nan-ch'üan.

19

Someone asked, "What do you mean by the mind that moment by moment does not differentiate?"

"The Master said, "The moment you ask such a question you show that differentiation has already taken place and that inherent nature and its manifestations have gone separate ways. Followers of the Way, make no mistake! The various phenomena in this world and other worlds are in all cases devoid of intrinsic nature. They are also devoid of any nature that manifests itself.[1] They are empty names, and the words used to describe them are likewise empty. But you insist on mistaking these idle names for reality. This is a great error. Even if something did exist, it would in all cases be no more than an environment that changes with what it depends on.

"There is the dependent condition called *bodhi,* the dependent condition of nirvana, the dependent condition of emancipation, the dependent condition of the threefold body, the dependent condition of environment and wisdom, the dependent condition of bodhisattva, the dependent condition of Buddha. You live in a land of changing dependent conditions—what is it you are looking for?

"And things like the Three Vehicles[2] and the twelve divisions of the scriptural teachings—they're all so much old toilet paper to wipe away filth. The Buddha is a phantom body, the patriarchs are nothing but old monks. You were born from women, weren't you?[3] If you seek the Buddha, you'll be seized by the Buddha devil. If you seek the patriarchs, you'll be fettered by the patriarch devil. As long as you seek something it can only lead to suffering. Better to do nothing.

"There are a bunch of bald-headed monks who tell students of the Way that the Buddha represents the ultimate goal, and that one must spend three *asamkhya kalpas* carrying out and fulfilling all the religious practices before one can gain complete understanding of the Way. Followers of the Way, if you say that the Buddha represents the ultimate goal, then why after living just eighty years did the Buddha lie down in the grove of sal trees in the city of Kushinagara and die?[4] Where is the Buddha now? From this we know clearly that he was no different from us in the realm of birth and death.

"You say that someone with the thirty-two features and the eighty auspicious characteristics is a buddha. But that must mean that a wheel-turning sage king is a Thus Come One.[5] So we know clearly that the Buddha is a phantom. A man of old said,

> The marks that fill the body of the Thus Come One
> were made to soothe worldly feelings.
> Lest people give way to nihilistic views,
> these empty names were postulated.
> As an expedient we talk of thirty-two features;
> the eighty characteristics are empty sounds.
> What has bodily shape is not the reality of
>   enlightenment.
> Its true form is without characteristics.[6]

"You say the Buddha has the six transcendental powers and that these are very wonderful.[7] But all the heavenly beings, the immortals, the *asuras,* and the powerful demons also have transcendental powers.[8] Does this mean they are buddhas? Followers of the Way, make no mistake. When the *asuras* fight against the god Indra and are defeated in battle, they lead their host of eighty-four thousand followers and all of them hide in a hollow filament of a lotus. Is this not miraculous?[9]

"But these examples I have cited are all powers that come from previous karma or that depend on something. The six transcendental powers of the Buddha are not like that. The Buddha can enter the realm of form without being misled by form, enter the realm of sound without being misled by sound, enter the realm of odor without being misled by odor, enter the realm of taste without being misled by taste, enter the realm of touch without being misled by touch, enter the realm of Dharma without being misled by Dharma. Therefore we can tell that these six things, form, sound, odor, taste, touch, and Dharma, are all empty of fixed characteristics. They can never bind or fetter this man of the Way who depends on nothing. Though his substance is defiled, made up of the five aggregates, he has the transcendental power of walking on the earth.[10]

"Followers of the Way, the true Buddha is without form, the true Dharma is without characteristics. You are striking poses and donning attitudes all because of a mere phantom. Even if in your seeking you got something, it would all be the work of wild fox spirits, certainly not the true Buddha. It would be the understanding of the non-Buddhists.

"A true student of the Way never concerns himself with the Buddha, never concerns himself with bodhisattvas or arhats, never concerns himself with the blessings of the threefold world. Far removed, alone and free, he is never entangled in things. Heaven and earth could turn upside down and he would not be perturbed. All the buddhas of the ten directions could appear before him and his mind would not feel an instant of joy, the three realms of hell[11] could suddenly confront him and his mind would not feel an instant of alarm. Why is he like this? Because he knows that all things in the phenomenal world are empty of characteristics. When conditions change, they come into existence; when there is no change, they do not exist. The threefold world is nothing but mind; the ten thousand phenomena are nothing but consciousness.[12] These 'dreams, phantoms, empty flowers—why trouble yourself trying to grasp them?'[13]

"There is only you, followers of the Way, this person in front of my eyes now listening to the Dharma, who enters fire without being burned, enters water without drowning, enters the three realms of hell as though strolling in a garden, enters the realms of the hungry ghosts and the animals but undergoes no punishment.[14] How can he do all this? Because he is not averse to anything.

> While you love sages, loathe common mortals,
> you're bobbing up and down in the sea of birth and
>   death.
> Earthly desires exist because of the mind;
> if no mind, what can earthly desires fix on?
> Don't labor to discriminate, to seize on marks;
> then without effort you'll gain the Way in a moment![15]

"If you rush off frantically on side roads, studying in hopes of gaining something, then for three *asamkhya kalpas* you will remain in the realm of birth and death. Better to do nothing, just sit in your seat here in the monastery with your legs crossed.

"Followers of the Way, when students come here from various regions and we have finished greeting one another as host and guest, the student will make some remark to test the teacher.[16] The student comes out with these tricky words and thrusts them into the teacher's face, as if to say, 'See if you can understand this!' If you were the teacher and realized that this was just an 'environment,'[17] and you grabbed it and threw it down a hole, then the student would act normal again and after that would ask for the teacher's instruction. The teacher would then snatch that up too and treat it as he did the earlier remark. The student then says, 'Very wise! A truly great teacher!' The teacher says, 'You certainly can't tell good from bad!'

"Again suppose the teacher comes out with a certain chunk of environment and dangles it in front of the student's face. The student sees through this and at every step acts the master, refusing to be misled by the environment. The teacher then reveals half of his body, whereupon the student gives a shout. The teacher now enters the place where there are all kinds of differences and distinctions, battering the student around with words. The student says, 'This old baldhead who can't tell good from bad!' The teacher exclaims in admiration, 'A true and proper follower of the Way!'

"There are some teachers around who can't distinguish crooked from straight. When a student comes and asks about *bodhi* or nirvana, about the threefold body or about environment and wisdom, those blind old teachers start explaining to the student. When the student curses at them, they pick up their stick and hit him, saying, 'Such rude language!' If you have a teacher like that, he lacks eyes to begin with. He has no cause to get angry at others.

"Then there is that bunch of baldheads who can't tell good from bad but point to the east, gesture to the west, love clear weather, love it when it rains, love this lamp or that pillar. Look and see how many hairs they have left in their eyebrows—and with good reason![18] If students fail to understand this, they'll become utterly bewitched in mind. Teachers like that are nothing but wild fox spirits, goblins. Good students will just give a little snicker and say, 'Blind old bald-heads trying to confuse and lead everybody in the world astray!'

"Followers of the Way, those who have left household life need to study the Way. I myself in past years turned my attention to the *vinaya*,[19] and I also delved into the sutras and treatises. But later I realized that these are just medicines to cure the sickness of the world, expositions of surface matters. So finally I tossed them aside and sought the Way through Ch'an practice. Later I encountered an excellent friend and teacher, and then my Dharma eye at last became keen and bright and for the first time I could judge the old reverends of the world and tell who was crooked and who was straight. But this understanding was not with me when my mother gave birth to me—I had to probe and polish and undergo experiences until one morning I could see clearly for myself.

"Followers of the Way, if you want to get the kind of understanding that accords with the Dharma, never be misled by others. Whether you're facing inward or facing outward, whatever you meet up with, just kill it! If you meet a buddha, kill the buddha. If you meet a patriarch, kill the patriarch. If you meet an arhat, kill the arhat. If you meet your parents, kill your parents. If you meet your kinfolk, kill your kinfolk. Then for the first time you will gain emancipation, will not be entangled with things, will pass freely anywhere you wish to go.[20]

"These students of the Way who come from all over—there's never been one of them who didn't appear before me depending on something. So I start right out by hitting them there. If they come with a raised hand, I hit the raised hand, if they come mouthing something, I hit them in the mouth, if they come making motions with their eyes, I hit them in the eye. I have yet to find one who comes alone and free—they're all caught up in the idle devices of the men of old.

"I don't have a particle of Dharma to give to anyone. All I have is cure for sickness, freedom from bondage. You followers of the Way from here and there, try coming to me without depending on anything. I would like to do some testing with you. But for ten years, for five seasons there's never been one such person! All I get are things stuck to stems, clinging to leaves, wraiths that inhabit bamboo or trees, wild fox spirits! They chew away frantically at every lump of shit they happen on.²¹ Blind fools! Shamelessly accepting alms from all the ten directions, they declare, 'I'm one who has left household life!' yet their understanding is like this.

"I tell you, there's no Buddha, no Dharma, no practice, no enlightenment. Yet you go off like this on side roads, trying to find something. Blind fools! Will you put another head on top of the one you have? What is it you lack?

"Followers of the Way, you who are carrying out your activities before my eyes are no different from the Buddha and the patriarchs. But you don't believe that and go searching for something outside. Make no mistake. There's no Dharma outside, and even what is on the inside can't be grasped. You get taken up with the words from my mouth, but it would be better if you stopped all that and did nothing. Things already under way, don't go on with them. Things not yet under way, don't let them get under way.²² That's better for you than ten years traveling around on pilgrimages.

"The way I see it, there's no call for anything special. Just act ordinary, put on your clothes, eat your rice, pass the time doing nothing. You who come from here and there, you all have a mind to do something. You search for Buddha, search for the Dharma, search for emancipation, search for a way to get out of the threefold world. Idiots, trying to get out of the threefold world! Where will you go?

"Buddha, patriarchs—these are just laudatory words and phrases.[23] Do you want to know what the threefold world is? It is nothing other than the mind-ground that you who are now listening to the Dharma are standing on. When you have a moment of greed in your mind, that is the world of desire.[24] When you have a moment of anger in your mind, that is the world of form. When you have a moment of ignorance in your mind, that is the world of formlessness. These are the pieces of furniture in your house.

"The threefold world does not announce, 'I am the threefold world.' Rather it's you, followers of the Way, who do so, this person here in front of my eyes who in marvelous fashion shines his torch on the ten thousand things and sizes up the world—it's *he* who assigns names to the threefold world.

"Fellow believers, this body made up of the four major elements has no permanence. Things like spleen and stomach, liver and gall, hair, nails, teeth are simply evidence that all phenomenal things are empty of fixed characteristics. When your mind has learned to cease its momentary seeking, this is dubbed the state of the *bodhi* tree. But while your mind is incapable of ceasing, this is dubbed the tree of ignorance. Ignorance has no fixed abode, ignorance has no beginning or end. As long as your mind is unable to cease its moment-by-moment activity, then you are up in the tree of ignorance. You enter among the six realms of existence and the creatures of four types of birth,[25] clothed in fur and with horns on your head. But if you can learn to cease, then you'll be in the world of the clean pure body. If not one thought arises, you'll be up in the *bodhi* tree, through your transcendental powers taking different forms in the threefold world, assuming any bodily shape you please, feasting on Dharma joy and meditation delight, illuminating things for yourself with the light from your own body.[26] Think of clothes and you'll be swathed in a thousand layers of fine silk, think of food and you'll be provided with a hundred delicacies.[27] And you will suffer no sudden illnesses. *Bodhi* has no fixed abode. That's why there's nothing to take hold of.

"Followers of the Way, the really first-rate fellow—what doubts does he have? Carrying out activities before my eyes—who is he anyway? Get hold of this thing and use it, but don't fix a label to it. This I call the Dark Meaning. When you can see it this way, you won't be averse to anything. A man of old said:

> The mind changes, following along with ten thousand
> environments;
> the way it changes is truly most mysterious.
> If you follow its flow and can perceive its nature,
> you will have neither joy nor sorrow.[28]

"Followers of the Way, in the view of the Ch'an school, dying and living proceed in proper order.[29] Those engaged in study must pay strict attention to this. Thus, when host and guest greet one another, there will be an exchange of remarks. Perhaps one party will respond to something and assume a certain form, or perhaps perform some activity with his entire body, perhaps try tricking the other by feigning delight or anger, perhaps reveal half of his body, perhaps come riding on a lion or riding on an elephant.[30]

"If the student truly knows what he is doing, he will give a shout and then first of all hold out a try of lacquer.[31] The teacher, failing to recognize this as a mere 'environment,' proceeds to climb up on the environment and begin striking poses or donning attitudes. The student gives a shout, but the teacher refuses to abandon his approach. In this case the sickness is located above the diaphragm and below the heart, where no cure can get at it. This is called the guest seeing through the host.[32]

"Or perhaps the teacher will not come out with any object of his own, but will wait for a question from the student and then snatch it away. The student, seeing his question snatched away, won't let go but holds on for dear life. This is a case of the host seeing through the guest.

"Perhaps there is a student who, responding with a clean pure environment, presents himself before the teacher. The teacher can tell this is just an environment and grabs it and throws it down a hole. The student says, 'A truly great teacher!' Instantly the teacher says, 'Hopeless—can't tell good from bad!' The student gives a low bow. This is called the host meeting up with a host.[33]

"Or there may be a student who puts a cangue [wooden collar] on his neck, binds himself in chains, and then comes before the teacher. The teacher proceeds to shackle him with another set of cangues and chains. The student is delighted, unaware of what has happened. This is called the guest meeting up with a guest.[34]

"Fellow believers, these examples I have cited are all meant to enable you to spy the devil, sort out what's improper, and learn to tell crooked from straight.

"Followers of the Way, it is very hard to know just how to proceed. The Dharma of the buddhas is profound and abstruse, though one can understand it to some degree. I spend all day explaining it in detail to you, but you students pay no attention. A thousand, ten thousand times you trample right over it with your feet, but you are sunk in darkness. It has no shape or form, yet its lone brightness gleams forth. But students don't have faith enough, and instead base their understanding on words and phrases. Their years pile up to half a hundred, and all they do is go off on side roads, carrying their dead corpses on their backs, racing all over the world with their load of baggage. The day will come when they'll have to pay for all those straw sandals they've worn out!

"Fellow believers, I tell you there is no Dharma to be found outside. But students don't understand me and immediately start looking inward for some explanation, sitting by the wall in meditation, pressing their tongues against the roof of their mouths, absolutely still, never moving, supposing this to be the Dharma of the buddhas taught by the patriarchs. What a mistake! If you take this unmoving, clean, and pure environment to be the right way, then you will be making ignorance the lord and master. A man of old said, 'Bottomless, inky black is the deep pit, truly a place to be feared!'[35] This is what he meant.

"But suppose you take motion to be the right way. Every plant and tree knows how to move back and forth, so does that mean they constitute the Way? To the degree that they move, it is due to the element air; to the degree that they do not move, it is the element earth. Neither their moving nor their not moving come from any nature innate in them.

"If you look toward the area of motion and try to grasp the truth there, it will take up its stand in the area of nonmotion, and if you look toward nonmotion and try to grasp it there, it will take up its stand in motion. It is like a fish hidden in a pond who now and then slaps the surface and leaps up.[36]

"Fellow believers, the moving and the unmoving are simply two types of environment. It is the man of the Way who depends on nothing who causes them to be in motion or to be motionless.

"When students come from here and there, I classify them into three categories according to their ability.[37] In such cases, if a student of less than middling ability comes to me, I snatch away the environment but leave him his existence. If a student of better than middling ability comes to me, I snatch away both environment and existence. If a student of truly superior ability comes to me, I do not snatch away anything, neither environment, nor existence, nor person. If a student appears whose understanding surpasses all these categories, then I deal with him with my whole body and take no account of his ability.

"Fellow believers, when it comes to this, where the student is exerting all his strength, not a breath of air can pass, and the whole thing may be over as swiftly as a flash of lightning or a spark from a flint. If the student so much as bats an eye, the whole relationship could be spoiled. Apply the mind and at once there's differentiation; rouse a thought and at once there's error.[38] The person who can understand this never ceases to be right before my eyes.

"Fellow believers, you lug your alms bag and this sack of shit that is your body and you rush off on side roads, looking for buddhas, looking for the Dharma. Right now, all this dashing and searching you're doing—do you know what it is you're looking for? It is vibrantly alive, yet has no root or stem. You can't gather it up, you can't scatter it to the winds. The more you search for it the farther away it gets. But don't search for it and it's right before your eyes, its miraculous sound always in your ears. But if you don't have faith, you'll spend your hundred years in wasted labor.

"Followers of the Way, in the space of an instant you may enter the Lotus Treasury world, enter the land of Vairochana, enter the land of emancipation, enter the land of transcendental powers, enter the clean pure land, enter the Dharma-realm, enter filth, enter purity, enter the state of common mortal, enter that of sage, enter the realm of hungry ghosts or of animals. But whatever place you journey to, wherever you hunt or search, nowhere will you find the living and the dead. All are mere empty names.

> Phantoms, illusions, empty flowers—
> why trouble yourself trying to grasp them?
> Gain, loss, right, wrong—
> throw them away at once![39]

"Followers of the Way, this Buddha-dharma of mine has come down to me in a very clear line, from Reverend Ma-yü, Reverend Tan-hsia, Reverend Tao-i, and the reverends Lu-shan and Shih-kung, a single road going all over the world.[40] But not a soul believes this, and everyone speaks slanderously of it.

"Reverend Tao-i's way of doing things was simple, direct, nothing mixed in.[41] He had three hundred, five hundred students, but not a one of them could see what he was getting at. Reverend Lu-shan was utterly free, true and correct, but whether he came at them with compliance or opposition, his students could never fathom what was going on, all being reduced to dumbfounded amazement. Reverend Tan-hsia toyed with a gem, concealing it, then revealing it.[42] The students who came to him all had to put up with curses. Ma-yü's way of doing things was as bitter as the bark of the Chinese cork tree; no one could get near him. The way Shih-kung went about it was to look for students by pointing an arrow at them; all who came to him were terrified.[43]

"The way I do things at present is to go about in a true and proper manner constructing and demolishing, toying and sporting with supernatural changes, entering every kind of environment but doing nothing wherever I am, not permitting the environment to pull me awry. Whoever comes to me seeking something, I immediately come out to size him up, but he doesn't recognize me. Then I put on various different robes. The student forms an understanding on that basis and begins to be drawn into my words.

"Hopeless, this blind baldhead without any eyes! He concentrates on the robe I'm wearing, noting whether it is blue, yellow, red, or white. If I strip off the robe and enter a clean pure environment, the student takes one look and is filled with delight and longing. If I throw that away too, the student becomes muddled in mind, racing around wildly in a distracted manner, exclaiming that now I have no robe at all! Then I turn to him and say, 'Do you know the person who wears this robe of mine?' Suddenly he turns his head, and then he knows me at last.

"Fellow believers, don't get so taken up with the robe! The robe can't move of itself—the person is the one who can put on the robe. There is a clean pure robe, there is a no-birth robe, a *bodhi* robe, a nirvana robe, a patriarch robe, a Buddha robe. Fellow believers, these sounds, names, words, phrases are all nothing but changes of robe. The sea of breath in the region below the navel stirs itself into motion, the teeth batter and mold it, and it comes out as a statement of an idea. So we know for certain that these are mere phantoms.

"Fellow believers, the karma of sounds and words finds outward expression, the objects of the mind are manifested within.[44] Because of mental processes thoughts are formed, but all of these are just robes. If you take the robe that a person is wearing to be the person's true identity, then though endless *kalpas* may pass, you will become proficient in robes only and will remain forever circling round in the threefold world, transmigrating in the realm of birth and death. Better to do nothing, 'to meet someone but not recognize him, talk with him but not know his name.'[45]

"The trouble with students these days is that they seize on words and form their understanding on that basis. In a big notebook they copy down the sayings of some worthless old fellow, wrapping it up in three layers, five layers of carrying cloth, not letting anyone else see it, calling it the 'Dark Meaning' and guarding it as something precious. What a mistake! Blind fools, what sort of juice do they expect to get out of old dried bones?

"There's a bunch of fellows who can't tell good from bad but poke around in the scriptural teachings, hazard a guess here and there, and come up with an idea in words, as though they took a lump of shit, mushed it around in their mouth, and then spat it out and passed it on to somebody else. They're like those people who play pass-the-word parlor games, wasting their whole lives like that. 'I've left household life!' they say, but if someone questions them about the Dharma of the buddhas, they clamp their mouths shut, speak not a syllable, their eyes like two blackened chimneys, their mouths drooping down like a bent carrying pole. Even when the time comes for Maitreya to make his appearance in the world, they'll still be off in some other world where they've been sent to suffer the torments of hell.[46]

"Fellow believers, you rush around frantically one place and another—what are you looking for, tramping till the soles of your feet are squashed flat? There is no Buddha to be sought, no Way to be carried out, no Dharma to be gained.

> Seeking outside for some Buddha possessing form —
> this hardly becomes you!
> If you wish to know your original mind,
> don't try to join with it, don't try to depart from it.[47]

"Followers of the Way, the true Buddha is without form, the true Way is without entity, the true Dharma is without characteristics. These three things mingle and blend, fusing together in one place. But because you fail to perceive this, you let yourselves be called creatures muddled by karma-created consciousness."

Notes

1. All things in the phenomenal world arise from and are dependent on various causes and conditions and are in a constant state of flux. They hence lack any intrinsic, or inherent nature, or any nature that manifests itself in fixed characteristics.

2. Three approaches or paths to enlightenment, that of the *shravaka,* or disciple of the Buddha, that of the *pratyekabuddha,* or self-enlightened being, and that of the bodhisattva.

3. Being born of a woman is an example of the kind of conditioned and dependent state that Lin-chi is talking about here.

4. The death of Shakyamuni Buddha as described in the scriptures. Kushinagara was in northeastern India near the Nepal border.

5. The thirty-two features and eighty auspicious characteristics are various unusual physical marks possessed by a buddha. They derive from earlier Indian thought, where they were said to distinguish a wheel-turning king or ideal ruler. *Tathagata,* or Thus Come One, is another name for a buddha.

6. From the "Hymn on the *Diamond Sutra*" by Fu Ta-shih (497–569).

7. The power of being anywhere at will, the power of seeing anything anywhere, the power of hearing any sound anywhere, the power of knowing the thoughts of all other minds, the power of knowing past lives, and the power of eradicating illusions. Only a buddha possesses all six, but the first five are also possessed by other types of beings.

8. The *asuras* are angry demons who in Indian mythology continually fight with the god Indra. The powerful demons are beings of a lower order who protect Buddhism.

9. Accounts of such legendary battles between Indra and the *asuras* are found in *Avatamsaka Sutra* 15 and other Buddhist works.

10. The five aggragates, which come together temporarily to form a human being, are matter, perception, conception, volition, and consciousness. The "power of walking on the earth" means the power to conduct oneself in a perfectly ordinary manner.

11. The hells of fire, of blood, and of knives.

12. The sentence is based on a passage in chapter 7 of the *Ch'eng-wei-shih lun,* a basic text of the Consciousness-Only School of Buddhism.

13. Quoted from the *Hsin-hsin ming,* or "Trust in the Mind," by the Third Patriarch Seng-ts'an.

14. Hell, the realm of hungry ghosts, and the realm of animals constitute the lowest of the six realms of existence. Ordinarily one is born in these three lower realms as a consequence of bad karma or evil acts done in previous existences, undergoing punishment there until one has worked off the effect of the bad karma.

15. This section is quoted from Pao-chih's "Hymns of the Mahayana" already quoted in section 11.

16. This section, known as "Lin-chi's Four Guests and Hosts,"

describes four types of interviews between a Ch'an master and a student, in which both parties seek to test and determine the other's level of understanding. In the first two interviews, both the student and the teacher demonstrate the correct approach. In most places, the text uses the term *shan-chih-shih,* or *good friend,* to designate the teacher, but for the sake of greater clarity I have translated it here as "teacher."

17. A certain pose or attitude the student assumes in order to draw the teacher out.

18. If one preaches an incorrect Dharma or preaches the Dharma in an incorrect manner, one is punished by having the hairs of his eyebrows fall out.

19. The section of the *Tripitaka* dealing with precepts and monastic discipline. The other two sections contain the sutras and treatises respectively.

20. All this talk of killing is of course intended merely to warn students not to be led astray by external goals or considerations, though the violence of Lin-chi's language has often shocked readers.

21. The sayings and teaching devices of the earlier masters.

22. The statement is fairly mysterious as it stands but presumably warns against sticking to mistaken conceptions or pursuits.

23. The translation is tentative. The text says, "words of praise and binding," an expression that has never been satisfactorily explained.

24. The threefold world is made up of the world of desire, the world of form, and the world of formlessness and is equivalent to the six realms of existence in which unenlightened beings transmigrate. Beings in the world of desire are dominated by desires for food, sex, etc. Beings in the world of form have material form but no desires. Beings in the world of formlessness are free from the restrictions of form but remain within the realm of the unenlightened and are subject to rebirth.

25. The six realms, as noted earlier, are those of hell, hungry

ghosts, animals, *asuras*, human beings, and heavenly beings. The four types of birth are birth from the womb, birth from an egg, birth from dampness, and birth by a process of transformation. Insects were believed to be born from dampness and heavenly beings and hell-dwellers to be born through a process of transformation.

26. Dharma joy and meditation delight are two of the five kinds of supermundane or nonmaterial foods by which enlightened beings are nourished.

27. Lin-chi is not suggesting that monks should take up luxurious ways, but is referring to conventional descriptions of the delights of the Buddhist Pure Land or paradise.

28. From the hymn by the Twenty-second Indian Patriarch Manorhita, as recorded in *Pao-lin chuan* 5.

29. The meaning is uncertain, but since Lin-chi has spoken earlier of the "living patriarch" or the "living thought of the patriarchs," and of killing buddhas, patriarchs, etc., it perhaps refers to the approval or rejection of certain ideas or attitudes. The paragraphs that follow, like those on pages 48–50 above, deal with four types of "guest and host" or student and teacher encounters.

30. The Bodhisattva Manjushri, who symbolizes wisdom, or the realm of the Absolute, is commonly depicted riding on a lion; the Bodhisattva Samantabhadra, symbolic of religious practice, or the realm of the relative, is shown riding on an elephant.

31. I.e., a trap that his opponent will get stuck in.

32. The student has seen through and bested the teacher. The example that follows represents the opposite situation.

33. That is, both student and teacher come out on top.

34. Both student and teacher have acted incorrectly.

35. The source of the quotation is unknown.

36. The simile is taken from the *Ta-ch'eng ch'eng-yeh lun,* the Chinese translation of Vasubandhu's *Karmasiddhiprakarana.*

37. This section, like section 10, deals with four procedures that Lin-chi uses with different types of students. In that section he spoke in terms of "environment" *(ching)* and "person" *(jen)*. Here he adds a third term, *fa,* which appears to be closely related to environment. Following Yanagida's interpretation, I translate it as "existence," though the meaning is uncertain. Iriya takes it to mean the student's concepts or ideas.

38. The sentence originates in the "Letter in Reply to Liu I-min" by Seng-chao (384–414).

39. Quoted from Seng-ts'an's "Trust in the Mind;" see note 13 above.

40. Ma-yü has appeared in section 2. Tan-hsia is Ch'an master T'ien-jan (738–823) of Mount Tan-hsia; Reverend Lu-shan is Ch'an master Chih-ch'ang of the Kuei-tsung Temple on Lu-shan, or Mount Lu; Shih-kung's name is Hui-tsang. Ma-yü, Chih-ch'ang, and Shih-kung were all students of Ma-tsu Tao-i.

41. Tao-i is Ma-tsu Tao-i (709–788).

42. *Ching-te ch'uan-teng lu* 30 records two poems by Tan-hsia entitled "Poems of Toying with a Gem."

43. Shih-kung had been a deer hunter before undergoing conversion to Buddhism and becoming a monk. When students came to him, he would fit an arrow to his bow, point it at them and say, "Look at the arrow!"

44. Quoted from the *Ta-ch'eng ch'eng-yeh lun.*

45. This seems to be an old saying; it appears also in the *Nan-ch'üan yü-yao,* a work containing the sayings of Nan-ch'üan.

46. Maitreya, the Buddha of the future, is destined to appear in this world to save all living beings 5 billion 670 million years after the death of Shakyamuni Buddha.

47. Quoted from a hymn by the Eighth Indian Patriarch Buddhanandi recorded in *Pao-lin chuan* 3. Since the original mind is identical with the Buddha-nature inherent in one, there is no need to make any special effort to "join" with it, nor of course to separate from it.

20

Someone asked, "What do you mean by the true Buddha, the true Dharma, and the true Way? Would you be good enough to explain to us?"

The Master said, "Buddha—this is the cleanness and purity of the mind. The Dharma—this is the shining brightness of the mind. The Way—this is the pure light that is never obstructed anywhere. The three are in fact one. All are empty names and have no true reality.

"The true and proper man of the Way from moment to moment never permits any interruption in his mind. When the great teacher Bodhidharma came from the west, he was simply looking for a man who would not be misled by others. Later the Second Patriarch encountered Bodhidharma, and after hearing one word, he understood. Then for the first time he realized that up to then he had been engaged in useless activity and striving.[1]

"My understanding today is no different from that of the patriarchs and buddhas. If you get it with the first phrase, you can be a teacher of the patriarchs and buddhas. If you get it with the second phrase, you can be a teacher of human and heavenly beings. If you get it with the third phrase, you can't even save yourself!"[2]

Notes

1. The Second Patriarch is Hui-k'o, who was active in the latter part of the sixth century. Lin-chi is probably referring to the famous story of how Hui-k'o asked for instruction from Bodhidharma but was constantly refused. In desperation Hui-k'o cut off his arm and presented it to Bodhidharma as proof of his determination, saying, "My mind is not at peace. I beg you

to pacify my mind!" Bodhidharma replied, "Bring me your mind and I'll pacify it for you." Hui-k'o said, "I've searched for my mind but I can't find it." "There," said Bodhidharma. "I've pacified your mind for you." This was presumably the "one word" that led Hui-k'o to enlightenment. The story is found in the *Tsu-t'ang chi, Ching-te ch'uan-teng lu,* and other Ch'an texts.

2. Whether this passage is related to the discussion of three phrases in section 9—and if so, just how—is uncertain.

21

Someone asked, "What was Bodhidharma's purpose in coming from the west?"[1]

The Master said, "If he had had a purpose, he wouldn't have been able to save even himself!"

The questioner said, "If he had no purpose, then how did the Second Patriarch manage to get the Dharma?"

The Master said, "Getting means not getting."

"If it means not getting," said the questioner, "then what do you mean by 'not getting'?"

The Master said, "You can't seem to stop your mind from racing around everywhere seeking something. That's why the patriarch said, 'Hopeless fellows—using their heads to look for their heads!'[2] You must right now turn your light around and shine it on yourselves, not go seeking somewhere else. Then you will understand that in body and mind you are no different from the patriarchs and buddhas, and that there is nothing to do. Do that and you may speak of 'getting the Dharma.'

"Fellow believers, at this time, having found it impossible

to refuse, I have been addressing you, putting forth a lot of trashy talk. But make no mistake! In my view, there are in fact no great number of principles to be grasped. If you want to use the thing, then use it. If you don't want to use it, then let it be.

"People here and there talk about the six rules and the ten thousand practices, supposing that these constitute the Dharma of the buddhas.[3] But I say that these are just adornments of the sect, the trappings of Buddhism. They are not the Dharma of the buddhas. You may observe the fasts and observe the precepts, or carry a dish of oil without spilling it, but if your Dharma eye is not wide open, then all you're doing is running up a big debt.[4] One day you'll have to pay for all the food wasted on you! Why do I say this? Because:

> If you embark on the Way but fail to master its
>   principles,
> then when you're reborn you must pay back the alms
>   of the believers.
> When the old man reaches the age of eighty-one,
> the tree will cease to grow fungus.[5]

"As for those who go off to live all alone on a solitary peak, eating only one meal a day at the hour of dawn, sitting in meditation for long periods without lying down, performing circumambulations six times a day—such persons are all just creating karma.[6] Then there are those who cast away their head and eyes, marrow and brains, their domains and cities, wives and children, elephants, horses, the seven precious things, throwing them all away.[7] People who think in that way are all inflicting pain on their body and mind, and in consequence will invite some kind of painful retribution. Better to do nothing, to be simple, direct, with nothing mixed in.

"If bodhisattvas, even those who have completed the ten stages of mind practice, were all to seek for the traces of such a follower of the Way, they could never find them. Therefore the heavenly beings rejoice, the gods of the earth stand guard with their legs, and the buddhas of the ten directions sing his praise. Why? Because this man of the Way who is now listening to the Dharma acts in a manner that leaves no traces."

Notes

1. A standard inquiry in Ch'an practice, similar to the question "What is the basic meaning of Buddhism?" in section 1.

2. The identity of the patriarch and source of the quotation are unknown.

3. See note 4, section 18. The ten thousand practices are various kinds of devotional acts.

4. Monks were expected to fast from noon until morning of the following day. The practice of filling a dish with oil and carrying it on the head for a given distance without spilling any is mentioned in *Ta-chih-tu lun* 15 and other Buddhist texts as an exercise for cultivating concentration of mind.

5. Lin-chi is quoting from a hymn by the Fifteenth Indian Patriarch Kanadeva recorded in *Pao-lin chuan* 3. According to the story told there, Kanadeva was traveling in central India when he came on an old man of seventy-nine and his son. In their garden was an old tree that had a delicious kind of fungus growing on it. The old man and his son ate the fungus, but it was invisible to everyone else. Kanadeva then composed his hymn in which he explained that in a former life the old man and his son had given alms to a certain monk, but the monk had failed to gain true enlightenment. As a consequence of his failure, he was reborn as the fungus on the tree so that in this way he might repay his debt to the old man and his son. Kanadeva predicted that when the old man reached the age of

eighty-one the debt would be repaid and the tree would cease to bear fungus. The son in time became a student of Kanadeva and succeeded him to become the Sixteenth Patriarch Rahulata.

6. Circumambulating a statue of the Buddha and paying obedience to it at six fixed times, three in the daytime and three in the night.

7. As the ruler did who is described in chapter 12 of the *Lotus Sutra*. The seven precious things in the *Lotus Sutra* are gold, silver, lapis lazuli, seashell, agate, pearl, and carnelian.

22

Someone said:

> The Great Universal Wisdom Excellence Buddha
> sat in the place of practice for ten *kalpas,*
> but the Dharma of the buddhas did not appear before him
> and he was unable to complete the Buddha Way.[1]

"I do not understand what this means. Would the Master be kind enough to explain?"

The Master said, " 'Great Universal' refers to you yourselves who, wherever you are, understand that the ten thousand things have no innate nature and no characteristics. Hence the name Great Universal. 'Wisdom Excellence' means that at all times and places one never doubts, never thinks one has gained a single thing. Hence the name Wisdom Excellence. 'Buddha' refers to the cleanness and purity of the mind, whose shining brightness penetrates throughout the Dharma-realm. So it gets the name *Buddha*. Sitting for ten *kalpas* in the place of practice refers to the ten *paramitas*.[2] The Dharma of the buddhas failing to appear before his eyes refers to the fact that the Buddha by nature is not subject to birth and the Dharma by nature is not subject to extinction. How then could it be the kind of thing that 'appears' before one? As for being unable to complete the Buddha Way, the Buddha doesn't need to do anything to make him a Buddha. A man of old said, 'The Buddha is eternally in this world but is not stained by the things of this world.'[3]

"Followers of the Way, if you want to attain Buddhahood, don't chase around after the ten thousand things. 'When mind arises, various kinds of things arise; when mind is extinguished, the various kinds of things are extinguished.'[4] 'If only the mind does not arise, then the ten thousand things will be blameless.'[5]

"Neither in this world nor in any other world is there any Buddha or any Dharma. There is nothing to appear before you, and nothing that is lost. Even if there were something, it would all be names, words, phrases, medicine to apply to the ills of little children to placate them, words dealing with mere surface matters. Moreover, these words and phrases do not declare themselves as words and phrases. It is you here before my eyes, who in clear and marvelous fashion observe, perceive, hear, know, and shine your torch, who assign all these various words and phrases.

"Fellow believers, only when you have committed the five crimes that bring on the hell of incessant suffering will you finally gain emancipation."[6]

Notes

1. The Great Universal Wisdom Excellence Buddha appears in chapter 7 of the *Lotus Sutra,* where it is said that he sat in the

place of religious practice for ten small *kalpas* but the Dharma, or doctrines of the buddhas, failed to appear before him. He does, however, in time gain enlightenment, and the point of the story is that he waits until other beings are ready to receive instruction before completing his own enlightenment, preaching, and then entering extinction. The Ch'an school from early times, however, has given the story a somewhat different interpretation, as will become evident here.

2. The six *paramitas* or religious practices listed in note 4, section 18, plus skill in expedient means, vows, power, and knowledge.

3. The words of the Bodhisattva Manjushri as found in the *Ju-lai chuang-yen chih-hui kuang-ming ju i-ch'ieh fo-ching-chieh ching.*

4. Quoted from the *Ta-ch'eng ch'i-hsin lun.* Hakeda translates the passage "When the [deluded] mind comes into being, then various conceptions (dharma) come to be; and when the [deluded] mind ceases to be, then the various conceptions cease to be." Yoshito S. Hakeda, *The Awakening of Faith* (New York: Columbia University Press, 1967), p. 49.

5. Quoted from Seng-ts'an's "Trust in the Mind."

6. The five deeds, or crimes, have been mentioned earlier in section 13. In section 23 Lin-chi gives his own interpretation of them, which is based in part on chapter 3 of the *Lankavatara Sutra.* Lin-chi's list of the five crimes differs somewhat from the usual one, and his interpretation turns the conventional meaning of the words completely upside down.

23

Someone asked, "What do you mean by the five crimes that bring on the hell of incessant suffering?"

The Master said, "Killing your father, injuring your mother, drawing blood from the Buddha's body, disrupting the harmony of the Monastic Order, burning the sutras and images—these are the five crimes that bring on the hell of incessant suffering."

The questioner said, "What is meant by the father?"

The Master said, "Ignorance is the father. When even for an instant your mind searches for some sign of arising and extinguishing but can find none, when it is like an echo responding to emptiness, when it is without activity wherever it is, this is called killing the father."

"What is meant by the mother?"

The Master said, "Greed is the mother. When even for an instant your mind, entering the world of desire and searching for greed, sees only that all phenomena are empty of characteristics, when it experiences no attachment anywhere, this is called injuring the mother."

"What is meant by drawing blood from the Buddha's body?"

The Master said, "If in the clean pure Dharma-realm your mind does not even for an instant begin to discriminate but instead sees complete darkness everywhere, this is drawing blood from the Buddha's body."

"What is meant by disrupting the harmony of the Monastic Order?"

The Master said, "If you properly understand that the bonds and entanglements of earthly desires are so much emptiness with no place to lean on, this is disrupting the harmony of the Monastic Order."

"What is meant by burning the sutras and images?"

The Master said, "When you can see the emptiness of causes and conditions, the emptiness of the mind, the emptiness of all phenomena, when the mind is every instant completely calm, far removed and doing nothing, this is burning the sutras and images. Fellow believers, if you can reach this kind of understanding, you will no longer be impeded by words such as *common mortal* or *sage*.

"Your minds instant by instant confront an empty fist, a pointing finger, and take it for some sort of reality, vainly thrashing around in the realm of senses, environments, phenomena. Or you think too little of yourselves, shrinking aside with the words, 'I'm just a common mortal, while he is a sage!'

"Bald-headed idiots! Why all this fluster? Will you put on a lion's skin and then yap like a jackal? First-rate fellows who don't draw a first-rate fellow's breath, you're unwilling to trust to what you have at home and instead go looking for something outside, letting yourselves become taken up with the idle words and phrases of the men of old, clinging to the shade, relying on sunshine,[1] never able to stand on your own. You encounter a certain environment and are swayed by it, you encounter a bit of dust and clutch at it, everywhere stirred and led astray, lacking any fixed standards of your own.

"Followers of the Way, don't be too taken up with my pronouncements either. Why? Because pronouncements are without basis or underpinning, something painted for a time on the empty sky, as in the simile of the painter with his colors.[2]

"Followers of the Way, don't take the Buddha to be some sort of ultimate goal. In my view he's more like the hole in a privy. Bodhisattvas and arhats are all so many cangues and chains, things for fettering people. Therefore Manjushri grasped his sword, ready to kill Gautama, and Angulimala, blade in hand, tried to do injury to Shakyamuni.³

"Followers of the Way, there is no Buddha to be gained, and the Three Vehicles, the five natures, the teaching of the perfect and immediate enlightenment are all simply medicines to cure diseases of the moment.⁴ None have any true reality. Even if they had, they would still all be mere shams, placards proclaiming superficial matters, so many words lined up, pronouncements of such kind.

"Followers of the Way, there are certain baldheads who turn all their efforts inward, seeking in this way to find some otherworldly truth. But they are completely mistaken! Seek the Buddha and you'll lose the Buddha. Seek the Way and you'll lose the Way. Seek the patriarchs and you'll lose the patriarchs.

"Fellow believers, don't mistake me! I don't care whether you understand the sutras and treatises. I don't care whether you are rulers or great statesmen. I don't care whether you can pour out torrents of eloquence. I don't care whether you display brilliant intellects. All I ask is that you have a true and proper understanding.

"Followers of the Way, even if you can understand a hundred sutras and treatises, you're not as good as one plain monk who does nothing. As soon as you acquire a little of such understanding, you start treating others with scorn and contempt, vying and struggling with them like so many *asuras,* blinded by the ignorance of self and others, forever creating karma that will send you to hell. You're like the monk Good Star who understood all the twelve divisions of the teachings but fell into hell alive, the earth unwilling to tolerate him.[5] Better to do nothing, to leave off all that.

> When you get hungry, eat your rice;
> when you get sleepy, close your eyes.
> Fools may laugh at me,
> but wise men will know what I mean.[6]

"Followers of the Way, don't search for anything in written words. The exertions of your mind will tire it out, you'll gulp cold air and gain nothing.[7] Better to realize that at every moment all is conditioned and without true birth, to go beyond the bodhisattvas of the Three Vehicle provisional doctrines.

"Fellow believers, don't dawdle your days away! In the past, before I had come to see things right, there was nothing but blackness all around me. But I knew that I shouldn't let the time slip by in vain, and so, belly all afire, mind in a rush, I raced all over in search of the Way. Later I was able to get help from others, so that finally I could do as I'm doing today, talking with you followers of the Way. As followers of the Way, let me urge you not to do what you are doing just for the sake of clothing and food. See how quickly the world goes by! A good friend and teacher is hard to find, as rarely met with as the *udumbara* flower.[8]

"You've heard here and there that there's this old fellow Lin-chi, and so you come here intending to confront him in debate and push him to the point where he can't answer. But when I come at students like that with my whole body, their eyes are wide open enough but their mouths can't utter a word. Dumbfounded, they have no idea how to answer me. Then I say to them, 'The trampling of a bull elephant is more than a donkey can stand!'[9]

"You go all around pointing to your chest, puffing out your sides, saying, '*I* understand Ch'an! *I* understand the Way!' But when two or three of you turn up here, you're completely helpless. For shame! With that body and mind of yours you go around everywhere flapping your two lips, hoodwinking the village people, but the day will come when you'll taste the iron cudgels of hell! You're not men who have left the household—you belong, all of you, in the realm of the *asuras!*

"The ultimate principles that make up the Way are not something to be thrashed out in contentious debate, clanging and banging to beat down the unbelievers. This thing handed down from the buddhas and patriarchs has no special meaning. If it were put in the form of verbal teachings, it would sink to the level of the teaching categories,[10] the Three Vehicles, the five natures, the conditions leading to birth as human and heavenly beings. But the teaching of the sudden and immediate enlightenment is not like that.[11] The Bodhisattva Good Treasures never went around searching anywhere.[12]

"Fellow believers, do not use your minds in a mistaken manner, but be like the sea that rejects the bodies of the dead.[13] While you continue to carry such dead bodies and go racing around the world with them, you only obstruct your own vision and create obstacles in your mind. When no clouds block the sun, the beautiful light of heaven shines everywhere. When no disease afflicts the eye, it does not see phantom flowers in the empty air.[14]

"Followers of the Way, if you wish to be always in accord with the Dharma, never give way to doubt. 'Spread it out and it fills the whole Dharma-realm, gather it up and it's tinier than a thread of hair.'[15] Its lone brightness gleaming forth, it has never lacked anything. 'The eye doesn't see it, the ear doesn't hear it.'[16] What shall we call this thing? A man of old said, 'Say something about a thing and already you're off the mark.'[17] You'll just have to see it for yourselves. What other way is there? But there's no end to this talk. Each of you, do your best! Thank you for your trouble."

Notes

1. The phrase is meant to describe a timid person who relies on the judgment of others, though the exact meaning is uncertain. Since the words translated as "shade" and "sunshine" are *yin* and *yang,* perhaps it refers to someone who relies on the pronouncements of the yin-yang diviners.

2. A reference to the passage in chapter 1 of the *Lankavatara Sutra* in which the Buddha compares his words to pictures painted in color on a wall by a painter and his disciples.

3. According to the story in *Pao-chi ching* 105, Manjushri, disturbed that the Buddha's preachings on the precepts were inspiring in his disciples a morbid sense of guilt, decided to prove to them that there was no such thing as evil karma by killing the Buddha (Gautama) with his own sword. Angulimala was a brigand who had vowed to make himself a headdress ornamented with the fingers of a hundred persons. He had almost completed the undertaking and was about to cut off the finger of his own mother when Shakyamuni confronted him. He attempted to attack Shakyamuni but was fended off and in the end became converted to the Buddha's teachings.

4. The Three Vehicles have appeared in section 19. The five natures, a doctrine of the Fa-hsiang school, divides human beings into five groups according to their inborn capacity for enlightenment. The teaching of the perfect and immediate enlightenment is the One Vehicle doctrine of Mahayan Buddhism, especially as expounded in the T'ien-t'ai and Hua-yen schools.

5. Good Star, or Sunakshatra, was a disciple of the Buddha who

was proficient at reciting the scriptures but could not understand their true meaning. As a result of his mistaken views he fell into hell while still alive. (See chapter 33 of the *Nirvana Sutra.*)

6. From the poem by Ming-tsan, or Lan-tsan, of Mount Nan-yüeh already quoted in section 13.

7. It has been suggested that the person "gulps cold air" because he is reading aloud, though the meaning is uncertain.

8. The *udumbara,* an imaginary plant often mentioned in Buddhist writings, blooms only once in three thousand years.

9. Lin-chi is quoting from the end of chapter 6 of the *Vimalakirti Sutra.*

10. The four types of teaching employed by the Buddha, namely, sudden or direct teaching, gradual teaching, secret teaching, and indeterminate teaching, in which the benefit derived from the teaching varies according to the capacity of the persons receiving it. It is a doctrine of the T'ien-t'ai school.

11. A few paragraphs earlier Lin-chi lumped the teaching of the sudden and immediate enlightenment together with the Three Vehicles and five natures as "medicine to cure diseases of the moment," so to translate in the way I have done here would seem to be unreasonable. However, there appears to be no other way to interpret the passage. Akizuki, Yanagida, and Iriya all take it the way I have.

12. Good Treasures, or Sudhana-shreshthi-daraka, described in the *Avatamsaka Sutra,* in the chapter called "Entering the Dharma-realm," is said to have traveled around visiting a total of fifty-three teachers in his search for enlightenment. Lin-chi is saying that in fact he never really went anywhere in his search because he had the potential for enlightenment, or the Buddha-nature, already within himself from the start.

13. As the sea casts up on the shore the bodies of the dead, so Lin-chi would have his students reject the idle words and teachings of the men of old, which are like so many dead bodies.

14. These last two sentences appear to be a quotation, but no source has as yet been identified.

15. From the *Chüeh-kuan lun* by Niu-t'ou Fa-jung (594–657) recorded in *Tsung-ching lu* 97.

16. From the *I-po-ko* or "Song of One Alms Bowl" by the Ch'an master Pei-tu recorded in *Ching-te ch'uan-teng lu* 30.

17. The words of Nan-yüeh Huai-jang (677–744) recorded in *Tsu-t'ang chi* 3.

PART THREE
Testing and Rating[1]

24

Huang-po had occasion to go into the temple kitchen. He asked the monk in charge of cooking rice, "What are you doing?"

The monk said, "I'm picking over the rice for the other monks."

Huang-po said, "How much do they eat in one day?"

"Two and a half piculs," said the monk.

"Isn't that too much?" said Huang-po.

"I'm only afraid it's not enough!" said the monk.

Huang-po immediately struck him a blow.

The monk mentioned the incident to the Master. The Master said, "For your sake I'll put this old fellow to the test!"

As soon as the Master had gone to Huang-po's quarters and was standing in attendance by him, Huang-po mentioned his earlier conversation with the monk in charge of cooking rice.

The Master said, "The monk didn't understand. I hope, Reverend, you'll be good enough to take his place and give us a turning word."[2] Then the Master said, "Isn't that too much rice?"

Huang-po said, "Why not say, 'Tomorrow you'll have a taste of it!'?"

The Master said, "Why say 'tomorrow?' Have a taste of it right now!" As soon as he had finished speaking, he gave Huang-po a slap.

Huang-po said, "This raving idiot, coming in here again and pulling the tiger's whiskers!"

The Master gave a shout and left the room.

Later Wei-shan asked Yang-shan, "What were those two worthy gentlemen up to?"[3]

Yang-shan said, "What do you think, Reverend?"

Wei-shan said, "When you bring up a son, you begin to understand a father's kindness."

Yang-shan said, "That's not it!"

Wei-shan said, "Well, what do you think?"

Yang-shan said, "It's just like bringing home a thief and losing everything in the house."

Notes

1. Encounters that test and reveal the degree of a person's religious understanding and experience and the correctness of the person's outlook.

2. An utterance that acts as a turning point in the situation, leading the listener to understanding.

3. Wei-shan Ling-yu (771–853) was a Dharma heir of Po-chang and a fellow student of Huang-po. He lived at Wei-shan, or Mount Wei, in T'an-chou in Hunan. Yang-shan Hui-chi (807–883), Wei-shan's disciple, lived at Yang-shan, or Mount Yang, in Yüan-chou in Kiangsi. They are the founders of the so-called Wei-Yang branch of Ch'an. These two appear as com-

mentators at the end of many of the episodes that follow. Note that in the Sasaki/Iriya translation of the *Lin-chi lu,* the name is romanized as Kuei-shan.

25

The Master asked a monk, "Where did you come from?"

The monk gave a shout.

The Master bowed slightly and motioned for him to sit down.

The monk was about to say something, whereupon the Master struck him a blow.

The Master saw a monk coming and held his fly whisk straight up.

The monk made a low bow, whereupon the Master struck him a blow.

The Master saw another monk coming and again held his fly whisk straight up.

The monk paid no attention, whereupon the Master struck him a blow as well.

26

One day the Master went with P'u-hua[1] to eat a meal at the home of a lay believer.

The Master said, "One hair swallows up the huge sea; one mustard seed holds Mount Sumeru.[2] Is this a manifestation of supernatural power, or is that just the way things have always been?"

P'u-hua kicked over his dinner tray.

The Master said, "Too coarse!"

P'u-hua said, "Where do you think you are, talking about what's coarse or what's fine!"

The following day the Master once again went with P'u-hua to eat a meal provided by a lay believer. He said, "I wonder how today's hospitality will compare with yesterday's?"

P'u-hua as before kicked over his dinner tray.

The Master said, "That's all right, to be sure, but it's too coarse!"

P'u-hua said, "Blind man! In the Buddha-dharma, what talk is there of coarse or fine?"

The Master stuck out his tongue in alarm.

Notes

1. P'u-hua was a Dharma heir of P'an-shan Pao-chi, though little is known of him outside of the episodes recorded here. He was the founder of the P'u-hua school.

2. Lin-chi's pronouncement on the hair and the mustard seed is based on a passage in chapter 6 of the *Vimalakirti Sutra*. The sutra deals with a lay patron of Buddhism much like the one who is here providing a meal for Lin-chi and P'u-hua, which

is perhaps why Lin-chi cites the passage. Mount Sumeru is the huge mountain that stands at the center of the world.

27

One day the Master was sitting with Ho-yang and Mu-t'a,[1] two elderly monks, around the fire pit in the dirt-floored part of the monks' hall. Someone took the opportunity to remark, "P'u-hua goes around the streets of town every day behaving like an idiot or a madman. I can't tell whether he's a common mortal or a sage."

Before the speaker had finished, P'u-hua came in.

The Master said, "Are you a common mortal or a sage?"

P'u-hua said, "You tell me, am I a common mortal or a sage?"

The Master gave a shout.

P'u-hua pointed with his finger and said, "Ho-yang is a new bride, Mu-t'a is an old Ch'an granny. Lin-chi is a little brat, but he's got an eye!"

The Master said, "This thief!"

P'u-hua said, "Thief! Thief!" and left the hall.

Note

1. The identity of these two monks is not known.

28

One day P'u-hua was in front of the monks' hall eating raw vegetables.

The Master saw him and said, "Exactly like a donkey!"

P'u-hua brayed like a donkey.

The Master said, "This thief!"

P'u-hua said, "Thief! Thief!" and walked away.

29

P'u-hua regularly went around the streets of the town ringing a hand bell and saying, "Come on the bright side and I'll hit you on the bright side. Come on the dark side and I'll hit you on the dark side. Come from four corners or eight directions and I'll hit you like a whirlwind. Come from the empty sky and I'll hit you like so many flails."

Because of this, the Master instructed his attendant to go and, as soon as P'u-hua had spoken in this way, to grab hold of him and say, "What will you do when I don't come in any of those ways?"

When the attendant had done so, P'u-hua pushed him away and said, "Tomorrow there's to be a meal at the Great Compassion Cloister."[1]

The attendant came back and reported this to the Master.

The Master said, "For some time now I've been suspicious of this fellow!"

Note

1. Ta-pei-yüan, a small temple in Chen-chou, later the residence of Lin-chi's disciple San-sheng.

30

An elderly monk came for an interview with the Master. Before he had finished with the customary greetings, he asked, "Would it be right to make a formal bow? Or would it be right to do without the bow?"

The Master gave a shout.

The elderly monk made a formal bow.

The Master said, "Quite some thief-in-the-grass!"

The elderly monk said, "Thief! Thief!" and left the room.

The Master said, "Better not think that that ends the matter!"

The head monk was standing in attendance. The Master said, "Were there any mistakes or not?"

The head monk said, "There were."

The Master said, "Was the guest mistaken? Or was the host mistaken?"

The head monk said, "Both were mistaken."

The Master said, "Where was the mistake?"

The head monk left the room.

The Master said, "Better not think that that ends the matter!"

Later a monk mentioned the incident to Nan-ch'üan.[1] Nan-ch'üan said, "Government horses trampling on each other."[2]

Notes

1. Usually identified as P'u-yüan (748–834) of Nan-ch'üan in Ch'ih-chou, a Dharma hear of Ma-tsu. But since P'u-yüan lived before Lin-chi's time, the identification is doubtful.

2. I.e., superior horses of the kind used by government officials.

31

The Master was entering an army encampment to attend a dinner when he saw one of the officers at the gate. He pointed to the bare wooden gatepost and said, "A common mortal or a sage?"

The officer had no reply.

The Master struck the gatepost and said, "Even if you managed a reply, it would still be just a wooden post!" With that he entered the camp.

32

The Master said to the director of temple business,[1] "Where have you been?"

The director said, "I've been to the district office to sell glutinous rice."[2]

The Master said, "Did you sell all of it?"

The director said, "Yes, I sold all of it."

The Master took his staff and drew a mark on the ground in front of him and said, "Can you sell this too?"

The director gave a shout.

The Master hit him.

When the supervisor of meals[3] happened along, the Master mentioned his earlier exchange.

The supervisor of meals said, "The director didn't understand your meaning, Reverend."

The Master said, "What about you?"

The supervisor made a low bow.

The Master hit him too.

Notes

1. The *yüan-chu,* a monk who manages secular affairs related to the temple.
2. In good years the government officials bought up supplies of surplus rice and stored it away for distribution in bad years.
3. The *tien-tso.*

33

A study director[1] came to see the Master. The Master said, "Study Director, what sutras or treatises are you lecturing on these days?"

The study director replied, "I'm a man of limited abilities, which I'm at present applying to the study of the *Treatise on the Hundred Dharmas.*"[2]

The Master said, "Suppose there were one man who understood the Three Vehicles and the twelve divisions of the teachings,[3] and another man who didn't understand the Three Vehicles and the twelve divisions of the teachings. Would they be the same or different?"

The study director said, "In understanding they would be the same. In not understanding they would be different."[4]

Lo-p'u,[5] who at the time was standing in attendance behind the Master, said, "Study Director, what kind of place do you take this for, talking of same and different!"

The Master turned his head and asked the attendant, "What do you think?"

The attendant gave a shout.

When the Master had returned from seeing off the study director, he said to the attendant, "Was it me you shouted at a moment ago?"

The attendant said, "Yes."

The Master struck him a blow.

Notes

1. See note 6, section 1.

2. The *Ta-ch'eng po-fa ming-men lun,* a work on the *Yogachara,* or Consciousness-Only doctrine, written by Vasubandhu (fifth century) and translated into Chinese by Hsüan-tsang (600–664). It is a basic text in the Fa-hsiang sect.

3. I.e., all the various writings and doctrines of Buddhism.

4. The statement is laconic. It may mean, "To one who understands, they are the same; to one who does not understand, they are different." In any event, the study director was attempting to give an answer that would avoid the appearance of dualistic thinking, but failed.

5. Yüan-an (834–898), who lived at Mount Lo-p'u in Feng-chou, a Dharma heir of Chia-shan Shan-hui.

34

The Master learned that the second Te-shan[1] was telling his students, "If you can speak, it's thirty blows, and if you can't speak, it's thirty blows!"

The Master instructed Lo-p'u, saying, "Go to his place and ask, 'If I can speak, why do I get thirty blows?' When he hits you, grab his stick, give him a jab, and see what he does then."

When Lo-p'u arrived at Te-shan's place, he followed the Master's instructions and asked the question. Te-shan hit him, whereupon he grabbed the stick and gave Te-shan a jab.

Te-shan returned to his own quarters.

Lo-p'u went back and reported to the Master what had happened.

The Master said, "For some time now I've been suspicious of this fellow! But however that may be, did you really get to see Te-shan?"[2]

Notes

1. Hsüan-chien (780–865), who lived in the Ku-te-ch'an-yüan at Te-shan, or Mount Te, in Lang-chou, was a Dharma heir of Lung-t'an Ch'ung-hsin. He was one of the most outstanding early Ch'an masters and was famous for striking his students with his stick; people commonly referred to "Lin-chi's shout and Te-shan's stick." He is called the second Te-shan to distinguish him from an earlier master of Te-shan, Tsung-yin, a Dharma heir of Ma-tsu.

2. That is, did you really understand what he was up to, or were you merely following instructions?

35

One day Constant Attendant Wang called on the Master and together they went to look at the monks' hall.

Constant Attendant Wang said, "This hallful of monks—do they read sutras perhaps?"

The Master said, "No, they don't read sutras."

"Do they perhaps learn how to meditate?" asked the Constant Attendant.

"No, they don't learn how to meditate," said the Master.

The Constant Attendant said, "If they don't read sutras and they don't learn how to meditate, what in fact *do* they do?"

The Master said, "We're training all of them to become buddhas and patriarchs."

The Constant Attendant said, "Gold dust may be precious, but if it gets in the eye it can blind.[1] What about it?"

The Master said, "And I always thought you were just an ordinary fellow!"

Note

1. A proverb of the time. In Ch'an, of course, any talk of becoming a buddha is taboo.

36

The Master said to Hsing-shan, "How about that white ox on the bare ground?"[1]

Hsing-shan said, "Moo, moo!"

The Master said, "Lost your voice?"

Hsing-shan said, "How about you, Reverend?"

The Master said, "This beast!"

Note

1. Hsing-shan is Chien-hung of Hsing-shan in Cho-chou, a Dharma heir of Yün-yen T'an-sheng (780–841). Lin-chi is referring to the parable in chapter 3 of the *Lotus Sutra,* in which a rich man, in order to lure his unwary children out of the burning house where they are playing, offers them a beautiful carriage drawn by a white ox, promising to give it to them after they get out of the house. The burning house represents the realm of delusion or ignorance, the carriage with the white ox is the One Vehicle of the Buddha's teaching as set forth in the *Lotus Sutra,* and the "bare ground" is the area outside the house, the realm of enlightenment.

37

The Master said to Lo-p'u, "Up to now, one man has used the stick, and another has used the shout. Which gets closer to it?"

Lo-p'u said, "Neither gets close to it!"

The Master said, "Then how would you get close to it?"

Lo-p'u gave a shout.

The Master struck him.

38

The Master saw a monk approaching and opened both hands and held them out.

The monk said nothing.

The Master said, "Do you understand?"

The monk said, "No, I don't."

The Master said, "This K'un-lun can't be broken open! Here's two coins for you."[1]

Note

1. K'un-lun is a mythical mountain west of China. Lin-chi means that the monk's stupidity is so monumental it is incapable of being overcome. The two coins represent the price of a pair of traveling sandals: the monk is being told to go elsewhere for instruction.

39

Ta-chüeh came to the Master for an interview.[1] The Master held his fly whisk upright.

Ta-chüeh spread his sitting cloth in preparation for a formal bow.[2]

The Master threw down his fly whisk.

Ta-chüeh folded up his sitting cloth and went to the monks' hall.

The other monks said, "This monk must be an old friend

of the Reverend, don't you suppose? He doesn't make a formal bow, and he doesn't get a taste of the stick either!"

The Master, hearing of this, had Ta-chüeh summoned. When Ta-chüeh appeared, the Master said, "The monks in my group are saying you haven't greeted me yet."

Ta-chüeh said, "How are you?" Then he returned and joined the other monks.

Notes

1. Some sources describe Ta-chüeh as a Dharma heir of Huang-po and hence a fellow disciple of Lin-chi, others as a disciple of Lin-chi. He lived at the Ta-chüeh Temple in Ta-ming Prefecture.
2. The sitting cloth, which is ordinarily folded up and carried over the shoulder, is spread on the ground when one makes a kowtow, or formal bow.

40

When Chao-chou[1] was traveling around, he came for an interview with the Master. The Master was just then washing his feet.

Chao-chou asked, "What did the Patriarch have in mind when he came from the west?"

The Master said, "As it happens, I'm just now washing my feet."

Chao-chou came close and made as though listening.

The Master said, "All right then, I'll throw out a second dipperful of dirty water!"[2]

With that, Chao-chou turned and left.

Notes

1. Ts'ung-shen (778–897) of the Kuan-yin-yüan in Chao-chou, a Dharma heir of Nan-ch'üan P'u-yüan.
2. The first dipperful was the answer, "As it happens, I'm just now washing my feet."

41

A certain distinguished monk named Ting[1] came to the Master for an interview and asked, "What is the basic meaning of Buddhism?"

The Master got down from his chair, grabbed hold of him and gave him a slap. Then he let him go.

Ting stood in a daze.

A monk standing nearby said, "Mr. Ting, why don't you make a bow?"

As Ting was making a formal bow, he suddenly had a great enlightenment.

Note

1. Nothing is known of him, though on the basis of this incident he has come to be regarded as a Dharma heir of Lin-chi. "Distinguished monk" is a translation of the honorific title *shang-tso,* or "upper seat."

42

Ma-yü came for an interview with the Master. He spread his sitting cloth and asked, "In the case of the twelve-faced Kuan-yin, which face is the real one?"[1]

The Master got down from his corded chair. With one hand he snatched up the sitting cloth and with the other he seized hold of Ma-yü and said, "The twelve-faced Kuan-yin—where'd it go to?"

Ma-yü twisted himself free and tried to sit down in the corded chair.[2]

The Master picked up his stick and hit him.

Ma-yü grabbed the stick and, each holding to one end of it, they went off to the Master's quarters.

Notes

1. Ma-yü has already appeared in section 2. The Bodhisattva Kuan-yin is often depicted as having multiple faces and arms, indicative of the bodhisattva's compassionate concern for others.
2. He was trying to assume the role of Kuan-yin.

43

The Master said to a monk, "At times my shout is like the precious sword of the Diamond King.[1] At times my shout is like a golden-haired lion crouching on the ground. At times my shout is like the search pole and the shadow grass.[2] At times my shout doesn't work like a shout at all. Do you understand?"

The monk started to answer, whereupon the Master gave a shout.

Notes

1. The sword of wisdom that cuts off all delusion.
2. According to commentators, the search pole has a feather on the end and is used to search out fish. The shadow grass is grass floating on the surface of the water that provides a shadowy place for fish to gather. That is, Lin-chi uses the shout to search out and test students the way the fisherman uses the pole and grass. This section is often referred to as "Lin-chi's Four Shouts."

44

The Master said to a nun, "Well come, or ill come?"[1]

The nun gave a shout.

The Master picked up his stick and said, "Speak then, speak!"

The nun shouted once more.

The Master struck her.

Note

1. In early Buddhism, novices entering a monastery were greeted with the words, "Well come, monk!" Lin-chi is playing on the conventional phrase.

45

Lung-ya[1] asked, "What did the Patriarch have in mind when he came from the west?"

The Master said, "Hand me the meditation board, please."[2]

Lung-ya handed the meditation board to the Master. The Master took it and hit Lung-ya with it.

Lung-ya said, "As far as hitting goes, you can hit me all right. But that's still not what the Patriarch had in mind."

Later Lung-ya arrived at Ts'ui-wei's place[3] and asked, "What did the Patriarch have in mind when he came from the west?"

Ts'ui-wei said, "Hand me the cushion, please."

Lung-ya handed the cushion to Ts'ui-wei. Ts'ui-wei took it and hit Lung-ya with it.

Lung-ya said, "As far as hitting goes, you can hit me all right. But that's still not what the Patriarch had in mind."

Later, when Lung-ya had settled down in a temple, a monk came to his room and requested special instruction, saying, "When you were traveling from place to place, Reverend, I've heard about how you had interviews with those two worthy old gentlemen. Do you approve of what they did or don't you?"

Lung-ya said, "As far as approving goes, I approve completely. But that's still not what the Patriarch had in mind."

Notes

1. Chü-tun (835–923), who lived at Mount Lung-ya in Hunan, a Dharma heir of Tung-shan Liang-chieh.

2. The meditation board is a backrest used to relieve fatigue when sitting in meditation. The conferring of such a backrest, like the conferring of the cushion mentioned later in the anecdote, was a mark of special honor for a student.

3. Ts'ui-wei is Wu-hsüeh, a Dharma heir of Tan-hsia T'ien-jan; he lived at Mount Chung-nan south of Ch'ang-an.

46

Ching-shan[1] had a group of five hundred monks under him, but few of them went for an interview and instruction.

Huang-po instructed the Master to go to Ching-shan's place. Then he said, "What do you intend to do when you get there?"

The Master said, "When I get there I'll think of some expedient."

The Master arrived at Ching-shan's place. Still dressed in his traveling clothes, he entered the Dharma Hall to see Ching-shan. Ching-shan had no sooner raised his head than the Master gave a shout.

Ching-shan made as though to open his mouth.

The Master shook out his sleeves and left.

One of the monks questioned Ching-shan, saying, "This monk just now—what sort of words of instruction did you give him that he shouted at you, Reverend?"

Ching-shan said, "This monk came from Huang-po's group. If you want to know, go ask him yourself."

Of Ching-shan's five hundred monks, over half left him and went elsewhere.

Note

1. Ching-shan, or Mount Ching, was an important Ch'an temple in Hang-chou-fu in Chekiang. In Sung times it was numbered among the Five Mountains, or key Ch'an monastic communities, and was headed by such eminent figures as Ta-hui and Hsü-t'ang. Who the head of it was at the time this incident took place we do not know. As so often in the text, the name of the place is used to stand for the Ch'an master in residence there.

47

One day P'u-hua went around the streets of the town begging people to give him a one-piece robe. But though people offered him one, he refused all their offers.

The Master sent the director of temple business out to buy a coffin. When P'u-hua returned to the temple, the Master said, "I've prepared this one-piece robe for you!"

P'u-hua shouldered the coffin and went off with it. He threaded his way through the streets of the town, calling out, "Lin-chi has prepared a one-piece robe for me! I'm going to the east gate to take leave of the world!"

The townspeople trooped after him, eager to see what would happen. P'u-hua said, "I'm not going to do it today. But tomorrow I'll go to the south gate and take leave of the world!"

He did this for three days, till no one believed him anymore. Then, on the fourth day, when no one was following or watching him, he went alone outside the city wall, lay down in the coffin, and asked a passerby to nail on the lid.

In no time, word of this spread abroad and the townspeople came scrambling. But when they opened the coffin, they found that all trace of his body had vanished. They could just catch the echo of his hand bell sounding sharp and clear in the sky before it faded away.

PART FOUR

Record of Activities

48

When the Master was first in Huang-po's group, he went about his activities in an earnest and straightforward manner. The head monk expressed admiration, saying, "Though he's still young, he's different from the others!" Then he asked, "How long have you been here?"

"Three years," said the Master.

The head monk said, "Have you been in to question the teacher yet?"

The Master said, "No, I haven't been in to ask questions. I don't know what to ask."

The head monk said, "Why don't you go ask the Reverend who heads this temple, 'What is the real basic meaning of the Buddha-dharma?' "

The Master went and asked, but before he had finished speaking, Huang-po struck him a blow.

When the Master returned from the interview, the head monk said, "How did the question go?"

The Master said, "Before I had even finished asking the question, the Reverend struck me. I don't understand."

The head monk said, "Just go ask him again."

The Master went and asked again, and again Huang-po hit him. In this way he went three times to ask his question and three times was struck.

The Master came to report to the head monk. "Thanks to your kind instruction, I've been able to question the Reverend. Three times I questioned him and three times he struck me. To my regret, I'm impeded by bad karma and can't grasp the profound meaning in all this. Now I'll be going on my way."

The head monk said, "If you're going, be sure to take leave of the Reverend."

The Master bowed low and withdrew.

The head monk went to see Huang-po before the Master could do so and said, "That young monk who came to question you has a lot of good sense. I hope you'll help him along. Later I'm sure he'll shape up into a fine big tree that will make cool shade for the people of the world."

When the Master came to take his leave, Huang-po said, "You mustn't think of going anywhere else—just go to Ta-yü's place by the river rapids in Kao-an.[1] He will surely explain things for you."

When the Master arrived at Ta-yü's place, Ta-yü asked, "Where have you come from?"

The Master said, "I've come from Huang-po's place."

Ta-yü said, "Did Huang-po have any words or phrases to teach you?"

The Master said, "I asked him three times what is the real basic meaning of the Buddha-dharma, and three times I was struck. I don't know whether I did something wrong or not."

Ta-yü said, "Huang-po is such a kind old grandmother,

wearing himself out on your account, and then you come here and ask whether you did something wrong or not!"

At these words, the Master experienced a great enlightenment. He said, "There really wasn't anything so hard about Huang-po's Buddha-dharma after all!"

Ta-yü seized hold of him and said, "This little bed-wetting devil! A minute ago asking if you did something wrong, and now you say there's nothing so hard about Huang-po's Buddha-dharma! What kind of truth do you think you've spied? Out with it! Out with it!"

The Master punched Ta-yü three times in the ribs with his fist.

Ta-yü let go of him and said, "Your teacher is Huang-po. You're no business of mine!"

The Master took leave of Ta-yü and returned to Huang-po. When Huang-po saw him coming, he said, "This fellow coming and going, coming and going—when will he ever have done with it?"

The Master said, "And it's all because of your grandmotherly kindness!" Then, when he had finished the customary greetings, he went and stood in attendance by Huang-po.

Huang-po said, "Where have you been?"

The Master said, "Following your kind instructions the other day, I went to visit Ta-yü."

Huang-po said, "Did Ta-yü have any words or phrases for you?"

The Master then related the conversation that had taken place between Ta-yü and himself.

Huang-po said, "If only I could get my hands on that fellow right now—I'd give him a real wallop!"

The Master said, "What's that you say you'll do? You can taste this right now!" With that he gave Huang-po a slap.

Huang-po said, "This raving idiot, coming back here and pulling the tiger's whiskers!"

The Master gave a shout.

Huang-po said, "Attendant, drag this raving idiot out of here and take him to the monks' hall!"

Later Wei-shan related this incident and asked Yang-shan, "At that time, was Lin-chi indebted to Ta-yü, or was he indebted to Huang-po?"

Yang-shan said, "He not only rode on the tiger's head, but he got to tweak the tiger's tail as well."

Note

1. A place on the Chin River in Jui-chou in Kiangsi. Ta-yü was a Dharma heir of Kuei-tsung Chih-ch'ang, but nothing else is known of him.

49

The Master was planting pines when Huang-po asked, "Why are you planting so many of them way off here in the mountains?"

The Master said, "First, to improve the appearance of the temple grounds. Second, to mark the road for people who come after."

When he had finished speaking, he took up his grub hoe and hacked at the ground three times.

Huang-po said, "That may be, but you've already tasted thirty blows of my stick!"

Again the Master took his hoe and hacked at the ground three times, blowing out his breath with a loud noise.

Huang-po said, "When my teaching line passes along to you, it will prosper greatly in the world."

Later Wei-shan mentioned these words to Yang-shan and said, "At that time, was Huang-po entrusting his teaching line to Lin-chi alone, or did he have someone else in mind?"

Yang-shan said, "There was someone else. But it was someone so far in the future that I'd hesitate to mention it to you, Reverend."

Wei-shan said, "That may be so, but I'd still like to know about it. Just try telling me what you can."

Yang-shan said, "The ruler points south and his commands are obeyed in Wu and Yüeh. But when they encounter the great wind, they cease." (A prophecy concerning Reverend Feng-hsüeh.)[1]

Note

1. The words in parentheses are a note appended to the text. According to the usual interpretation of Yang-shan's cryptic utterance, the word *south (nan)* refers to Nan-yüan Hui-yung (d. ca. 950), the fourth patriarch of Lin-chi's line; and the mention of Wu and Yüeh refers to his Dharma heir Feng-hsüeh Yen-chao (896–973), who came from the Wu-Yüeh region. The prediction concerning the great wind suggests that under Feng-hsüeh's direction the Ch'an teachings will flourish greatly.

50

The Master was standing in attendance at Te-shan's side.[1] Te-shan said, "I'm tired today!"

The Master said, "What's this old fellow doing talking in his sleep?"

Te-shan struck the Master a blow.

The Master grabbed the chair Te-shan was sitting on and turned it over.

Te-shan let the matter end there.

Note

1. Te-shan has appeared earlier in section 34.

51

The Master was out working with the other monks hoeing the fields when he saw Huang-po coming. Using his grub hoe for a staff, he stood leaning on it.

Huang-po said, "This fellow's tired, eh?"

The Master said, "I haven't even lifted up my hoe—why should I be tired?"

Huang-po struck him a blow. The Master grabbed hold of Huang-po's stick and gave it a shove, knocking him over.

Huang-po called to the *wei-na,* "*Wei-na,* help me up!"[1]

The *wei-na* came forward to help him. "Reverend," he said, "why do you put up with such rudeness from this raving idiot?"

As soon as Huang-po got to his feet, he struck the *wei-na* a blow.

The Master, hoeing the ground, said, "Other places they cremate them, but at our place we bury them all alive!"

Later Wei-shan asked Yang-shan, "When Huang-po hit the *wei-na,* what was that about?"

Yang-shan said, "When the real thief runs away, the man who was chasing him gets walloped."

Note

1. The *wei-na* is an official who directs temple affairs. *Wei-na* is a Chinese transcription of the Sanskrit word *karmadāna.*

52

One day the Master was sitting in meditation in front of the monks' hall when he saw Huang-po coming. Immediately he shut his eyes. Huang-po made as though he were frightened and then returned to his living quarters.

The Master followed him to his quarters and apologized. The head monk was standing in attendance at Huang-po's side.

Huang-po said, "This monk may be young, but he understands about this business!"

The head monk said, "Old Reverend, you must not have your feet on the ground if you give your approval to this young fellow!"

Huang-po gave himself a slap on the mouth.

The head monk said, "As long as you understand, it's all right."

53

The Master was in the monks' hall sleeping. Huang-po came in to look around and rapped on the meditation platform with his stick.

The Master raised his head, but when he saw it was Huang-po, he went back to sleep.

Huang-po rapped again on the platform and then went to the upper part of the hall.[1] There he saw the head monk sitting in meditation. He said, "That young monk in the lower hall is sitting in meditation. What are you doing here lost in daydreams!"

The head monk said, "This old fellow—what's he up to!"

Huang-po rapped on the platform and then left the hall.

Later Wei-shan asked Yang-shan, "When Huang-po came into the monks' hall, what was all that about?"

Yang-shan said, "Two winners in one throw."[2]

Notes

1. The meditation hall faced east. The meditation platform on the north side of the hall was called the upper hall, that on the south side, the lower hall.
2. The point of the episode is that all activities—sitting, walking, sleeping, etc.—are a form of meditation when properly done.

54

One day when the group was going out to work in the fields, the Master walked along behind.

Huang-po turned his head and, seeing the Master empty-handed, asked, "Where's your grub hoe?"

The Master said, "Somebody went off with it."[1]

Huang-po said, "Come over here. I want to work this matter out with you."

The Master went over to where he was. Huang-po stood his hoe upright and said, "When it comes to this, no one in the world can take hold of it and lift it up."

The Master proceeded to grab the hoe in his hand and stand it upright. "Then what's it doing in *my* hand?" he said.

Huang-po said, "Today there was somebody who did a good day's work!" Then he went back to the monastery.

Later Wei-shan asked Yang-shan, "If the hoe was in Huang-po's hand, how could it have been snatched away by Lin-chi?"

Yang-shan said, "The thief's a petty fellow, but clever beyond his betters."[2]

Notes

1. From here on the language becomes metaphorical, words such as "somebody" or "this" taking on a special significance.
2. A proverb of the time.

55

The Master was sent by Huang-po to deliver a letter to Wei-shan's place.[1] At that time Yang-shan was in charge of receiving visitors. After taking the letter, he said, "This is Huang-po's. Now where is yours?"

The Master gave him a slap.

Yang-shan seized hold of his hand and said, "Brother, if you know that much, that ends the matter." Together they went in to see Wei-shan.

Wei-shan asked, "How many monks has my brother Huang-po?"

The Master said, "Seven hundred monks."

Wei-shan said, "Who is the leader among them?"

The Master said, "He handed a letter to you just now!" Then the Master asked Wei-shan, "Reverend, how many monks do you have here?"

Wei-shan said, "Fifteen hundred monks."

The Master said, "That's a lot!"

Wei-shan said, "Brother Huang-po has quite a few too."

When the Master took his leave of Wei-shan, Yang-shan escorted him out of the room and said, "If later you go to the north, you'll find a place to live."

The Master said, "Why should that be?"

Yang-shan said, "Just go. Later there will be a man who will surely help you, brother. But this man—he'll have a head but no tail, a beginning but no end."

Later, when the Master arrived in Chen-chou, he found that P'u-hua was already living there. When the Master began teaching, P'u-hua assisted him. But before the Master had lived there for long, P'u-hua took leave of the world, body and all.

Note

1. Traveling from Mount Huang-po in Kiangsi to Mount Wei in Hunan, a distance of 700 li, or about 230 miles.

56

The Master came to Huang-po's place in the middle of the summer session.[1] There he saw Huang-po reading sutras.

The Master said, "I thought you must be quite some person. But now I find you're just an old reverend who munches on black beans!"[2]

After staying a few days, the Master prepared to take leave.

Huang-po said, "You broke the rules by coming in the summer. Now you're going to leave without finishing out the session?"

The Master said, "I just came for a short time to pay my respects, Reverend."

Huang-po struck him a blow and drove him out.

After the Master had gone a few miles, he began to have doubts about the matter, so he went back and finished out the summer session.

One day the Master came to take leave of Huang-po. Huang-po asked, "Where will you go?"

The Master said, "If not Ho-nan, then I'll go back to Ho-pei."

Huang-po struck him. The Master grabbed Huang-po's arm and slapped him with the palm of his hand.

Huang-po gave a loud laugh and then called to his attendant, "Bring Master Po-chang's meditation board and arm-rest!"[3]

The Master said, "Attendant, bring me some fire!"[4]

Huang-po said, "You're right, of course. But take them with you anyway. Later on, you can use them to sit on the tongues of the men of the world!"

Later Wei-shan questioned Yang-shan about this. "Did Lin-chi betray Huang-po's expectations or not?"

Yang-shan said, "No, he didn't."

Wei-shan said, "What do you think?"

Yang-shan said, "Once you understand your obligations, you'll know how to repay them."

Wei-shan said, "Were there any cases like this among the men of old times?"

Yang-shan said, "There were. But it happened so long ago in the past that I'd hesitate to mention it to you, Reverend."

Wei-shan said, "That may be, but I'd still like to know. Just tell me what you can."

Yang-shan said, "At the gathering where the Buddha preached the *Shuramgama Sutra,* Ananda praised him, saying, 'You take this profound mind and present it to all the numberless lands of the universe. This is what is called repaying the obligations of the Buddha!'[5] Isn't this an example of how to repay obligations?"

"You're right, you're right!" said Wei-shan. "When one's understanding is only equal to that of his teacher, he diminishes the teacher's merit by half. Only when his understanding surpasses that of his teacher is he worthy of carrying on the line."

Notes

1. The summer session at Ch'an temples usually lasted from the sixteenth day of the fourth lunar month to the fifteenth day of

the seventh month. During this period, monks were not supposed to travel around, so Lin-chi was breaking the rules by arriving in the middle of the summer session.

2. The act of reading a text in Chinese is likened to eating black beans, since the characters look something like beans.

3. Po-chang Huai-hai (720–814) was Huang-po's teacher. Huang-po is signifying that he has passed Po-chang's teachings on to Lin-chi.

4. Indicating that he intends to burn the meditation board and armrest.

5. Quoted from chapter 3 of the *Shuramgama Sutra*. Ananda was Shakyamuni's favorite disciple and his personal attendant.

57

The Master arrived at Bodhidharma's memorial tower.[1] The keeper of the tower said, "Will Your Reverence bow first to the Buddha, or first to the Patriarch?"

The Master said, "I will not bow to the Buddha, or to the Patriarch either."

The keeper of the tower said, "Has Your Reverence some grudge against the Buddha and the Patriarch?"

The Master shook out his sleeves and left.

Note

1. The memorial tower marked the grave of Bodhidharma, the First Patriarch, who was believed to have introduced the Ch'an teachings to China. It was at the temple called Ting-lin-ssu at Mount Hsiung-erh in Ho-nan.

58

When the Master was traveling around on foot, he came to Lung-kuang's place.[1]

Lung-kuang ascended the hall to lecture. The Master stepped forward and asked, "Without unsheathing a weapon, how is it possible to win?"

Lung-kuang straightened up in his seat.[2]

The Master said, "My great good friend, surely you're not without some means to help me!"

Lung-kuang, his eyes glaring, sighed loudly.

The Master pointed a finger at him and said, "Old fellow, you certainly lost out today!"

Notes

1. Nothing is known about Lung-kuang.
2. This gesture was intended as an answer.

59

When the Master arrived at San-feng, Reverend P'ing[1] asked, "Where have you come from?"

"From Huang-po," the Master said.

P'ing said, "What kind of words and phrases did Huang-po have for you?"

The Master said, "The golden ox last night fell into the furnace. Since then no one's seen a trace of it."

P'ing said, "In the golden wind of autumn he blows a jade flute. But who is it that understands the tune?"

The Master said, "He passed right through the ten-thousandfold barrier, doesn't even linger in the pure heights of heaven."

P'ing said, "Your query is far too lofty!"

The Master said, "A dragon gave birth to a golden phoenix that smashed through the turquoise of the sky."

P'ing said, "Sit down a while and drink your tea."

Later he asked, "Where else have you been recently?"

The Master said, "Lung-kuang."

P'ing said, "How is Lung-kuang these days?"

The Master got up and left.[2]

Notes

1. Nothing is known of Reverend P'ing of Mount San-feng.

2. As an example of how the cryptic utterances of these exchanges are interpreted, I give here the explanation of this passage found in Akizuki's notes, which is based on traditional Japanese interpretations of the text. There is no guarantee that this is what Lin-chi and Reverend P'ing intended by their remarks, but it is at least a possible and indeed plausible interpretation of the exchange.

   P'ing said, "What kind of words and phrases did Huang-po have for your?"

   The Master said, "The golden ox last night fell into the furnace. Since then no one's seen a trace of it." ("Huang-po taught me the highest level of truth where all dualisms disappear.")

   P'ing said, "In the golden wind of autumn he blows a jade flute. But who is it that understands the tune?" ("Huang-po's teachings are indeed lofty. But can you really understand them?")

   The Master said, "He passed right through the ten-thousandfold barrier, doesn't even linger in the pure heights of heaven." ("I have not only understood them, but I have gone beyond them!")

P'ing said, "Your query is far too lofty!" ("You are getting out of hand!")

The Master said, "A dragon gave birth to a golden phoenix that smashed through the turquoise of the sky." ("The dragon, Huang-po, has produced a phoenix, Lin-chi, who reaches the highest level.")

P'ing said, "Sit down a while and drink your tea." (P'ing gives up the battle.)

60

When the Master arrived at Ta-tz'u's place,[1] Ta-tz'u was sitting in his quarters.

The Master said, "When you sit up straight here in your room, what is it like?"

Ta-tz'u said, "Cold pine, a single hue, different for a thousand years. Country oldsters plucking blossoms, spring in ten thousand lands."

The Master said, "Now as in the past, forever transcending the Perfect Wisdom state. But the Three Mountains are locked away behind ten-thousandfold barriers."[2]

Ta-tz'u gave a shout.

The Master also gave a shout.

Ta-tz'u said, "What's that?"

The Master shook out his sleeves and left.

Notes

1. Huan-chung (780–862) of Mount Ta-tz'u in Hang-chou, a Dharma heir of Po-chang Huai-hai.

2. *Ta-yüan-ching-chih,* the Great Perfect Mirror–Wisdom, is one of the four types of wisdom, that which, like a mirror, reflects all things in their true state. The Three Mountains are generally taken to mean the three islands in the eastern sea where, according to traditional Chinese lore, the immortals dwell. But one commentator suggests they refer to a three-peaked mountain called Three Mountains on the Yangtze southwest of Nanking mentioned in a poem by Li Po (701–762) entitled "Climbing the Phoenix Terrace in Chin-ling."

61

When the Master arrived at Hua-yen's place in Hsiang-chou,[1] Hua-yen was propped on his staff, bent over as though sleeping.

The Master said, "Old Reverend, what do you mean by dozing?"

Hua-yen said, "A first-rate Ch'an man is obviously not the same as others."

The Master said, "Attendant, make some tea and bring it for the Reverend to drink."

Hua-yen then summoned the *wei-na.* "See that this gentleman is seated in the third seat."[2]

Notes

1. Probably the Hua-yen-yüan at Lu-men-shan in Hsiang-chou, Hupeh; we do not know who was the master in residence there at this time.

2. On the title *wei-na,* see note 1, section 51. The third seat is a place of distinction in the meditation hall, occupied by a monk who helps in the instruction of the other monks. Hua-yen re-

fers to Lin-chi by the honorific term *shang-tso,* or "upper seat."

62

When the Master arrived at Ts'ui-feng's place,[1] Ts'ui-feng asked, "Where did you come from?"

"From Huang-po," the Master said.

Ts'ui-feng said, "What words and phrases does Huang-po use to instruct people?"

The Master said, "Huang-po has no words or phrases."

Ts'ui-feng said, "Why doesn't he have any?"

The Master said, "Even if he had any, they wouldn't be the sort of thing to mention."

Ts'ui-feng said, "Try mentioning them anyway."

The Master said, "An arrow streaks through the western sky."

Note

1. The identity of Ts'ui-feng is not known.

63

When the Master arrived at Hsiang-t'ien's place,[1] he asked, "Not a common mortal, not a sage—please, Master, speak quickly!"

Hsiang-t'ien said, "I am just as you see me."

The Master gave a shout and then said, "All you baldheads—what kind of food do you hope to find in a place like this?"[2]

Notes

1. The identity of Hsiang-t'ien is not known.
2. These words are addressed to Hsiang-t'ien's followers.

64

When the Master arrived at Ming-hua's place, Ming-hua[1] said, "Coming and going, coming and going—what is it all about?"

"Just tramping around wearing out my straw sandals," said the Master.

Ming-hua said, "In the end, what is it for?"

"This old man doesn't even know how to talk!" said the Master.

Note

1. The identity of Ming-hua is not known.

65

The Master went to see Feng-lin.[1] On the way he met an old woman. "Off somewhere?" she asked.

"Off to Feng-lin," the Master said.

"I think you'll find that Feng-lin isn't in right now," the old woman said.

"Off somewhere?" said the Master.

The old woman walked away.

The Master called after her. She turned her head, where-upon the Master walked away.[2]

Notes

1. The identity of Feng-lin is not known.
2. Some texts read *ta,* "struck," instead of *hsing,* "walked away," here and in the preceding paragraph. But it seems unlikely that the old woman and Lin-chi would exchange blows.

66

When the Master arrived at Feng-lin's place, Feng-lin said, "There's something I'd like to ask about—may I?"

The Master said, "How can you gouge out the flesh and inflict a wound?"

Feng-lin said, "The sea moon shines, no shadows any-where, yet the swimming fish by themselves manage to lose their way."

The Master said, "Since the sea moon is without shadow, how can the swimming fish lose their way?"

Feng-lin said, "Watch the wind and you'll know what kind of waves will rise up. Sporting on the water, a country boat spreads its sail."

The Master said, "The solitary moon shines alone, river and mountains hushed. I give one shout of laughter and heaven and earth take fright."

Feng-lin said, "It's all right for you to use your three-inch tongue to dazzle heaven and earth. But try saying one phrase about the situation we face right now!"

The Master said, "If you meet a master swordsman on the road, you have to give up your sword. But when the other person is not a real poet, never present him with a poem."[1]

Feng-lin at that point gave up.

The Master then wrote a poem:

> The Great Way knows no like or different;
> it can go west or east.
> Sparks from a flint can't overtake it,
> streaks of lightning would never reach that far.

Wei-shan asked Yang-shan, "If 'sparks from a flint can't overtake it, streaks of lightning would never reach that far,' then how have all the wise men from ages past been able to teach others?"

Yang-shan said, "What do you think, Reverend?"

Wei-shan said, "It's just that no words or explanations ever get at the true meaning."[2]

Yang-shan said, "Not so!"

Wei-shan said, "Well, what do you think?"

Yang-shan said, "Officially not a needle is allowed to pass, but privately whole carts and horses get through!"

Notes

1. A common saying of the time.
2. A quotation from the *Shuramgama Sutra*, chapter 3.

67

When the Master arrived at Chin-niu's place,[1] Chin-niu saw him coming and, placing his staff across his knees, sat down squarely in the middle of the gate.

The Master rapped with his hand three times on the staff and then went off to the monks' hall and sat down in the number one seat.

Chin-niu came to look at him and said, "There are appropriate ceremonies to be observed when a guest and host meet. Where did you come from, sir, that you behave in this outrageous manner!"

The Master said, "Old Reverend, what's that you say?"

Chin-niu was about to open his mouth when the Master struck him a blow. Chin-niu made as though he were falling down, whereupon the Master struck him again.

Chin-niu said, "Today is not my day!"

Wei-shan asked Yang-shan, "With these two worthy old gentlemen, was there any winning and losing, or wasn't there?"

Yang-shan said, "As for winning, they won all the way. And as for losing, they lost all the way."[2]

Notes

1. He was perhaps a Dharma heir of Ma-tsu, though nothing is known of him for certain.
2. Or, following the more common interpretation, "As for winning, they both won. And as for losing, they both lost."

68

When the Master was about to pass away, he sat up straight in his seat and said, "After I am gone, you must not destroy my True Dharma Eye!"[1]

San-sheng[2] came forward and said, "Who would dare to destroy the Master's True Dharma Eye?"

The Master said, "Afterward, if someone should ask you about it, what would you say to that person?"

San-sheng gave a shout.

The Master said, "Who knows? My True Dharma Eye may well be destroyed by this blind donkey here!"

When he had finished speaking, he remained seated upright and entered nirvana.

Notes

1. *Cheng-fa yen-tsang* (J. *shōbōgenzō*), literally, "the eye and treasury of the True Dharma," the basic truth of Buddhism.
2. San-sheng Hui-jan, who after Lin-chi's death helped to compile the *Lin-chi lu*.

69

Pagoda Inscription of Ch'an Master Lin-chi Hui-chao[1]

The Master's personal name was I-hsüan and he was a native of Nan-hua in Ts'ao-chou.[2] His surname was Hsing. As a child he displayed unusual qualities, and when he grew older he was known for his filial devotion. Later, when he shaved his head and received full ordination in the precepts, he took up residence in the lecture halls, assiduously studying the *vinaya* and reading widely and diligently in the sutras and treatises.

Suddenly he sighed and said, "These are mere medicines and expedients to save the world. They are not that doctrine that has been separately transmitted outside the scriptural teachings!" He thereupon changed his robes and set out to journey to other parts. At first he received instruction from Huang-po, and later he visited Ta-yü. The words exchanged with them on those occasions are recorded in the "Record of Activities."

After receiving the Dharma seal from Huang-po, he went to the Ho-pei region and became the head of a small monastery overlooking the Hu-t'o River outside the southeast corner of the walled city of Chen-chou. The name Lin-chi, which means "overlooking the ford," derives from the location of the temple.

At this time P'u-hua was already living in the city, mingling with the populace and behaving like a madman, and no one could tell whether he was a common mortal or a sage. When the Master arrived, P'u-hua assisted him, but just when the Master's teachings began to flourish, P'u-hua took leave of the world, body and all. This fitted perfectly with the prediction made earlier by Yang-shan, the "Little Shakyamuni."[3]

There happened to be an outbreak of fighting in the area and the Master had to abandon his temple. But Grand Commandant Mei Chün-ho gave up his own house within the city walls and turned it into a temple, hanging up the Lin-chi plaque there and inviting the Master to take up residence.[4]

Later the Master shook out his robes and went south until he reached Ho Prefecture. The head of the prefecture, Constant Attendant Wang, welcomed him and treated him as his teacher.[5] He had not been there long when he moved to the Hsing-hua Temple in Ta-ming Prefecture, where he resided in the eastern hall.[6]

The Master was not ill, but one day he suddenly arranged his robes, sat down in his seat and, when he had finished exchanging remarks with San-sheng, quietly passed away. The time was the eighth year of the Hsien-t'ung era of the T'ang, a year with the cyclical sign *ting-hai* [867], the tenth day of the first month.[7] His disciples buried the Master's body whole and erected a pagoda in the northwest corner of the Ta-ming prefectural capital. By imperial command he was given the posthumous name Ch'an Master Hui-chao [Wise and Illumined] and the pagoda was given the name Ch'eng-ling [Pure and Holy].[8]

Pressing my palms together and bowing my head, I have recorded this brief outline of the Master's life.

Respectfully written by Yen-chao, Dharma heir of the Master, residing in the Pao-shou Temple in Chen-chou.[9]

Text collated by Ts'un-chiang, Dharma heir of the Master, residing in the Hsing-hua Temple in Ta-ming Prefecture.[10]

Notes

1. These words in parentheses have been added from the *Ku-tsun-su yü-lu* version of the text.

2. In present day Yen-chou-fu in Shantung.

3. See section 55 above. The *Yang-shan yü-lu* and other texts mention that Yang-shan was referred to as Hsiao Shih-chia or "Little Shakyamuni."

4. Attempts have often been made to identify Mei, or Mo, Chün-ho with Mo Chün-ho (the Mo written with a different character), a military leader who went to the aid of Wang Yung, the

prince of Chao, when he was attacked in 893, but recent research has demonstrated that this is chronologically impossible.

5. Traditionally it has been supposed that "Ho Prefecture" refers to Ho-nan Prefecture, the region south of the Yellow River where Lin-chi was born, and that Wang, the head of the prefecture, is the same as the Wang mentioned in sections 1 and 2. But since Lin-chi has already known the official Wang during his stay in Chen-chou, why is he shown here meeting him for the first time? Yanagida believes that Ho refers to the prefecture of Ho-chung in present-day Shansi, and that the statement about being welcomed by the official Wang should simply be ignored. See his article cited in note 1 of the introduction.

6. Ta-ming is Wei-chou in Hopeh. The Hsing-hua-ssu was the temple of Lin-chi's Dharma heir Ts'un-chiang.

7. Other sources such as *Tsu-t'ang chi* 19, *Sung Kao-seng chuan* 12, etc., give the date of his death as the tenth day of the fourth month of Hsien-t'ung seven (866).

8. The sources mentioned in note 7 give the name of the pagoda as Ch'eng-hsü [Pure and Empty].

9. The sources mentioned in note 7 refer to a "Reverend Chao of the Pao-shou [the Pao written with a different character from that used in the text] of Chen-chou," but whether this is the same person as Yen-chao is not certain.

10. This probably refers to the collation of the entire text of the *Lin-chi lu*.

Appendix

THE FOLLOWING TWO SECTIONS, which are found in the version of the *Lin-chi lu* in Ming editions of the *Ku-tsun-su yü-lu,* are sometimes included in editions of the *Lin-chi lu*. They are found, for example, on pages 44–45 and 152–153 of Iriya's text and translation. The fact that they are not found in the Sung edition of the *Ku-tsun-su yü-lu* makes them somewhat suspect. The first section is clearly related to a phrase in Ma Fang's preface to the text, though which came first is difficult to determine. The second is closely linked to material found in section 55 of the *Lin-chi lu*. I have translated them here for the reference of readers, though in the case of the first I have very little idea what the meaning may be. The first section is often referred to as "Lin-chi's Four Illuminations and Actions." See note 13 to Ma Fang's preface. "Illumination" refers to the teacher's appraisal of the student's understanding, and "action" to the action he takes on the basis of that appraisal.

The Master instructed the group, saying: "Sometimes illumination comes first and action afterward. Sometimes action comes first and illumination afterward. Sometimes illumination and action are simultaneous. Sometimes illumination and action are not simultaneous.

131

"When illumination comes first and action afterward, then the person is present. When action comes first and illumination afterward, then the Dharma[1] is present. When illumination and action are simultaneous, it's like driving away the plowman's ox, snatching food from a starving person, cracking bones and extracting the marrow, giving a painful poke with a needle or an awl. When illumination and action are not simultaneous, there are questions and answers, guest and host are established, water gets mixed with mud, in response to movements measures are taken. If the person is really outstanding, then even before a problem arises he'll rouse himself and be on his way. But still it needs another little push.

When the Master first met P'u-hua, he said, "When I was in the south delivering a letter to Wei-shan's place, I learned that you were already living here and waiting for me to come. Now that I've come, I can get you to help me. I'm hoping now to propagate the teachings of Huang-po's line. You must by all means help me to do so."

P'u-hua said, "Good-bye now," and went on his way. Later, when K'o-fu[2] arrived, the Master made the same request. K'o-fu likewise said, "Good-bye now," and went on his way.

Three days later, when P'u-hua came to inquire how the Master was, he said, "Reverend, why did you say what you did the other day?"

The Master picked up his stick, hit P'u-hua, and drove him out.

Three days later, K'o-fu also came to inquire how the Master was, and then asked, "Reverend, why did you hit P'u-hua the other day?"

The Master once more picked up his stick, hit K'o-fu, and drove him out.

Notes

1. Or, if this passage is related to that in section 19 of the *Lin-chi lu,* perhaps the word *fa* here should be translated as "existence." See note 37, section 19.
2. A Dharma heir of Lin-chi.

Glossary

Sanskrit names and terms are given in parentheses with full diacritical marks when this form differs from the simplified one in which the word appears in the translation. Skt. = Sanskrit; Ch. = Chinese; J. = Japanese.

ANANDA *(Ānanda)*   One of Shakyamuni's ten major disciples. He accompanied Shakyamuni as his personal attendant for many years and was the Buddha's favorite disciple.

ANGULIMALA *(Aṅgulimāla)*   A brigand whose name means "necklace of fingers" and who had set out to kill one hundred persons and make a necklace of their fingers. He had killed ninety-nine and was about to kill his own mother for the hundredth when he encountered Shakyamuni, who rebuked him and in time made him his follower.

ARHAT   A "worthy," a follower of Hinayana, or Lesser Vehicle, Buddhism who has overcome the passions and gained release from the cycle of birth and death. The seventh-highest path of existence in the Ten Worlds (see below).

ASURAS   In Indian mythology, a class of angry demons who are constantly engaged in warfare with the god Indra. The fourth-highest realm of existence in the Ten Worlds.

AVATAMSAKA *(Avataṃsaka)* SUTRA   (Ch. *Hua-yen ching,* J. *Kegonkyō*) An important Mahayana sutra, often referred to in English as the *Flower Garland Sutra.*

BODHI   Buddhist wisdom or enlightenment.

135

BODHIDHARMA   An Indian monk who went to China in the late fifth or early sixth century and introduced the Ch'an teachings there. According to legend, he arrived in south China and later made his way to the north, where he spent nine years practicing meditation with his face to the wall. He is honored as the First Patriarch of Chinese Ch'an Buddhism.

BODHISATTVA   A being who has vowed to attain Buddhahood and who out of compassion constantly works to assist others to do so. Some sutras divide bodhisattva practice into fifty-two stages, from initial resolution to the final realization of enlightenment. The realm, or path, of the bodhisattva is the ninth of the Ten Worlds.

CH'AN (J. *Zen*)   A Chinese term used to represent the Sanskrit word *dhyāna,* or meditation. Later used to designate the school of Buddhism introduced to China by Bodhidharma, which placed great emphasis on meditation practice.

DHARMA (Ch. *fa,* J. *hō*)   The Law, or body, of Buddhist teachings. In Ch'an Buddhism the teachings are handed down from the teacher or Ch'an master to the disciples. Those who receive the full body of the teachings of a particular master and are certified as fully qualified to carry them on are known as the master's Dharma heirs.

DHARMA-REALM (Skt. *Dharma-dhātu*)   1. The realm or sphere of the ultimate reality. 2. The entire universe.

GAUTAMA   The family name of Shakyamuni, another name for Shakyamuni Buddha.

GOOD STAR (Skt. *Sunakṣātra*)   A disciple of Shakyamuni described in chapter 33 of the *Nirvana Sutra.* Though proficient in reciting the scriptures, he could not understand their true meaning and instead gave himself up to mistaken views. As a result he fell into hell while still alive.

GOOD TREASURES (Skt. *Sudhana-śreṣṭhi-dāraka*)   A bodhisattva described in the Gaṇḍa-vyūha chapter, "Entering the Dharma-realm," in the *Avatamsaka Sutra.* He was called Good Treasures because at the time of his birth gold, silver, and other treasures appeared of themselves in his home. He traveled about visiting fifty-three bodhisattvas in his search for enlightenment, gaining it at last from the bodhisattva Samantabhadra (see below).

KALPA   In Indian thought, an extremely long period of time. Lin-chi often speaks of an *asaṃkhya kalpa, asaṃkhya* being an ancient Indian numerical unit indicating an uncountably large number.

KUAN-YIN (Skt. *Avalokiteśvara,* J. *Kannon*)   An important bodhisattva in Mahayana Buddhism, symbolic of compassion, who assumes many different forms in order to save people from danger and suffering. Originally a male figure, in Chinese and Japanese art the bodhisattva is commonly depicted in female form. The bodhisattva is often shown as having eleven faces and a thousand arms in order to heed and assist all believers.

LANKAVATARA *(Laṅkāvatāra)* SUTRA (Ch. *Leng-chia ching,* J. *Ryōgakyō*)   A Mahayana sutra that was important in early Ch'an thought.

LESSER VEHICLE   English translation of the term *Hinayana,* by which the followers of Mahayana, or Great Vehicle, Buddhism designate the teachings of earlier Buddhism.

MAITREYA   An important bodhisattva in Mahayana Buddhism who has been designated by Shakyamuni to become the Buddha of the future. He will appear in the world 5 billion 670 million years after Shakyamuni's death.

MANJUSHRI *(Mañjuśrī)*   A prominent bodhisattva in Mahayana Buddhism, depicted in the sutras as a disciple of Shakyamuni and regarded as the symbol of the perfection of wisdom. He is usually shown riding a lion. In China his cult, centered at Mount Wu-t'ai in Shansi, was very important in T'ang times.

NIRVANA *(nirvāṇa)*   Final liberation from suffering, the goal of Buddhist aspiration and practice, where the highest wisdom is attained.

PARAMITA *(pāramitā)* The *paramitas* are practices that Mahayana bodhisattvas are expected to carry out in order to attain enlightenment. Reference is usually made to the six *paramitas,* namely, almsgiving, keeping of the precepts, forbearance, assiduousness or diligence in practice, meditation, and wisdom. At one point Lin-chi refers to ten *paramitas;* these are the six listed above plus skill in expedient means, vows, power, and knowledge.

PATRIARCH A term usually used in the *Lin-chi lu* to designate the patriarchs of the Ch'an school in China, of whom the most important were Bodhidharma, the First Patriarch of Ch'an in China, and Hui-neng, the Sixth Patriarch. The Ch'an school also speaks of twenty-eight Indian patriarchs who transmitted the teachings down through the ages from Shakyamuni to Bodhidharma.

PRATYEKABUDDHA A self-enlightened being or solitary sage, one who has gained enlightenment through his own efforts but makes no attempt to enlighten others. The eighth highest of the Ten Worlds.

SAMANTABHADRA A leading bodhisattva in Mahayana Buddhism, known in China as P'u-hsien and in Japan as Fugen. Symbolic of religious practice, he is usually depicted riding on a white elephant. In China his cult was centered on Mount Omei in Szechwan.

SHAKYAMUNI *(Śākyamuni)* The "Sage of the Shakyas," the name of the Buddha of our present era, who lived and taught in India around the sixth or fifth century BCE.

SHUNYATĀ *(śūnyatā)* Emptiness or Void (Ch. *k'ung,* J. *kū*), the Mahayana concept of nondualism.

SHURAMGAMA *(Śūraṃgama)* SUTRA (Ch. *Leng-yen ching,* J. *Ryōgonkyō*) An important Mahayana sutra often quoted in other Mahayana writings and apparently widely read in ancient India.

TEN WORLDS Ten realms of existence into which all living beings are divided in the Mahayana world concept. The first six, the "six paths," represent the realms of ordinary or unenlightened beings. In ascending order these are (1) hell, (2) hungry ghosts, (3) beasts, (4) *asuras,* (5) human beings, and (6) heavenly beings. Above these are the realms of enlightened beings, namely, (7) arhats, (8) *pratyekabuddhas,* (9) bodhisattvas, and (10) buddhas.

THREEFOLD BODY   A fundamental doctrine in Mahayana Buddhism that teaches that there are three aspects in which the person of a buddha may be viewed. First is the *Dharmakāya,* or Essence-body, the Buddha as pure Dharma or Suchness. Second is the *Sambhogakāya,* or Bliss-body, sometimes called the Reward-body, the Buddha as endowed with infinite attributes of bliss gained through practice as a bodhisattva. Third is the *Nirmaṇakāya,* or Transformation-body, how the buddha appears to ordinary believers when manifesting in the world in order to save them.

THREEFOLD WORLD   The world of desire, the world of form, and the world of formlessness. These three compose the world inhabited by unenlightened beings who transmigrate within the six paths or realms of existence.

THREE VEHICLES   The three types of teachings expounded for persons pursuing the path of the arhat, the *pratyekabuddha,* and the bodhisattva respectively. Mahayana scriptures such as the *Lotus Sutra* urge believers to set aside these three paths or teachings and pursue the One Vehicle teachings that lead to Buddhahood.

THUS COME ONE (Skt. *Tathāgata,* Ch. *Ju-lai,* J. *Nyorai*)   An epithet or term for a buddha.

TRIPITAKA   The canon of Buddhist scriptures. It is made up of three large divisions, the sutras, the *vinaya* texts, or rules of monastic discipline, and the treatises, or commentaries.

TWELVE DIVISIONS   Another name for the Buddhist scriptures as a whole. The texts are classified into twelve groups on the basis of their style of expression.

VAIROCHANA *(Vairocana)* A Buddha who figures prominently in the *Avatamsaka, Mahavairochana,* and other Mahayana sutras.

VIMALAKIRTI *(Vimalakirtī)* A wealthy Indian merchant who lived in Shakyamuni's time and had a profound understanding of the Buddha's teachings. Symbolic of the ideal lay believer, he is the central figure in the *Vimalakirti Sutra.*

WEI-NA A Chinese term used to designate an official who directs the administrative affairs of a temple.

YAJNADATTA *(Yajñadatta)* A young man of good family who thought he had lost his head, from a story in the *Shuramgama Sutra.*